SACRAMENTO PUBLIC LIBRARY
828 "I" Street
Sacramento, CA 95814
10/17

Here we meet a skilled master se
theological concepts and explainii
and practical, Horton's book proves genuinely inviting to the newcomer.
Learn from a master who is not afraid to put things simply and clearly.

—KELLY M. KAPIC, Professor of Theological Studies,
Covenant College, author of *God So Loved He Gave*

When I was in college, I needed an introduction to what Christians
believe about redemption—not what my own denomination believed
but what all Christians have always believed. A favorite professor told
me to read John Stott's *Basic Christianity*, and that book was a gift of
God for me. I still have my underlined copy. In *Core Christianity* you
have a similar book, one fit for a new generation the way Stott's was for
his generation. Here you will find what Christians believe about what
most matters about the most important topics. You might need an extra
copy to give to those who, like me many years ago, need an introduction
to core Christianity.

—SCOT MCKNIGHT, Julius R. Mantey
Professor of New Testament, Northern Seminary

I read straight through this solid book on the central truths of the
Christian faith and was impressed. But when I searched the text for
some of the standard technical terms of theology, I found that Horton
had managed to deliver the whole message in simple, nontechnical language. Then I was doubly impressed. This is a very useful little book.

—FRED S' Professor,
Torrev ' Jniversity

QG 03-14-17

CORE CHRISTIANITY

FINDING

YOURSELF IN

GOD'S STORY

MICHAEL HORTON

ZONDERVAN

Core Christianity
Copyright © 2016 by Michael Horton

This title is also available as a Zondervan ebook.
Visit www.zondervan.com/ebooks.

This title is also available as a Zondervan audio book.
Visit www.zondervan.com/fm.

Requests for information should be addressed to:

Zondervan, 3900 Sparks Dr. SE, Grand Rapids, Michigan 49546

Library of Congress Cataloging-in-Publication Data

Names: Horton, Michael Scott.
Title: Core Christianity : finding yourself in God's story / Michael Horton.
Description: Grand Rapids, MI : Zondervan, Grand Rapids, [2015] | Includes
    bibliographical references and index.
Identifiers: LCCN 2015038319 | ISBN 9780310525066 (softcover)
Subjects: LCSH: Theology, Doctrinal—Popular works. | Christian life.
Classification: LCC BT77 .H637 2015 | DDC 230—dc23 LC record available at http://
    lccn.loc.gov/2015038319

Scripture quotations are taken from The Holy Bible, New International Version®, NIV®.
Copyright © 1973, 1978, 1984, 2011 by Biblica, Inc.® Used by permission of Zondervan.
All rights reserved worldwide. www.Zondervan.com. The "NIV" and "New International
Version" are trademarks registered in the United States Patent and Trademark Office
by Biblica, Inc.®

Any Internet addresses (websites, blogs, etc.) and telephone numbers in this book are
offered as a resource. They are not intended in any way to be or imply an endorsement
by Zondervan, nor does Zondervan vouch for the content of these sites and numbers
for the life of this book.

All rights reserved. No part of this publication may be reproduced, stored in a retrieval
system, or transmitted in any form or by any means—electronic, mechanical, photocopy,
recording, or any other—except for brief quotations in printed reviews, without the
prior permission of the publisher.

Cover design: MetaLeap Creative
Interior art: MetaLeap Creative, © 2015 by Michael Horton
Interior design: Kait Lamphere

Printed in the United States of America

16 17 18 19 20 21 22 23 24 25 26 /QG/ 15 14 13 12 11 10 9 8 7 6 5 4 3 2 1

To James, Adam, Matt, and Olivia

CONTENTS

ACKNOWLEDGMENTS

THE FRUIT OF MANY YEARS and many collaborations, I cannot hope to include all of the people to whom I am grateful for this book. I have benefited once again from working with the team at Zondervan. Ryan Pazdur has once again guided me through the process from conception to editing and Christopher Beetham suggested critical improvements. Our team at White Horse Inn, led by Mark Green, has been of inestimable value in developing the concept and giving input along the way. I am particularly grateful to Lydia Brownback, a longtime friend and collaborator, who lent her remarkable editing skills to the project, although I take responsibility for any remaining errors. Finally, I am grateful to my wife Lisa and to James, Adam, Matthew, and Olivia. They not only indulge me in my passion but exemplify in their own lives that growth in grace that has encouraged and challenged me along the way.

GETTING STARTED

GOD'S STORY AND OURS, OR WHY DOCTRINE MATTERS

YOU BROUGHT YOUR THREE-YEAR-OLD into the emergency room for what you thought was a common cold. Within an hour you learn that it's a fatal disease. Your first thought is to pray. Why? Because you believe in a God who intervenes in this world. Your act of prayer assumes you believe that the world—including you and your daughter—wasn't self-created and that it isn't self-sustaining. There is a God who transcends the world but also created it. He is good and all-powerful. Your prayer reveals that you have a specific worldview, even if you may not be aware of the details or the reasons for your belief, and that worldview arises from a particular story—the story of God as told in the Bible.

But you have a neighbor who had a similar experience. He doesn't pray because he doesn't believe in God. Nature plus chance—for him, that's all there is. In his mind there is no author of the story. Or, in the absence of God, he is writing his own story with himself as the lead character. So then, how can he even conclude that his daughter's weakness is somehow a *problem*? Of course, he experiences it as a problem. But his experience contradicts what he says he believes about reality. If evolution has wired things for the survival of the fittest, his daughter probably *should* die. It's a thinning out of the herd so she can't pass along her faulty DNA to the rest of the race.

The story we believe determines which of these approaches to life we will take. It is not just a belief here or there as if we could just lift lines at random from the narrative. Rather, it is the story as a whole, from the opening scene until the last page. We experience and live out roles that fit in the broader narrative.

For the most part we take the story we're living in for granted. Both believers and unbelievers don't always know why they think, feel, and live the way they do. It's just assumed. When you first learned to ride a bike, you focused on the handlebars and pedals. Or when you started piano lessons, you concentrated on your fingers and the keys. And when people experience a major conversion of some sort, they are typically aware of why and how it happens.

When it comes to life-altering conversions, some people do not come to realize that the story in which they have been operating no longer makes sense, but a new one does. Others can recall a life-altering experience but cannot explain the story they left behind or the one that now shapes their identity, hopes, fears, and actions.

A lot of Christians take their story—the narratives that give rise to their beliefs—for granted. They pray, go to church, perhaps even read their Bible. But they might be stymied if a stranger asked them to explain what they believe and why they believe it. The purpose of this book is to help you understand the reason for your hope as a Christian so that you can invite others into the conversation. This book is for those who are tired of being starring characters in their own life movie. You want to be written into God's unfolding drama. But where do you start? Before we embark on this journey, I want to make a case briefly for why it is so important in the first place. Let me challenge you to consider the following questions that go right to the heart of where we live.

1. *Why should I be interested in Christian doctrine?* We study things we care about. We pursue an education to work in a particular field. People invest enormous amounts of time and energy in sports, culture, business, child-rearing, learning a new technology, and various hobbies. It's all about desire. What do we really love? What are the most important things in life?

In some cases, doctrine seems irrelevant because there is a firewall between faith and reason, believing and thinking. "I just believe," people say, but what do they believe? And why? The average person on the street relegates religion to the realm of irrational feelings, not facts, and dismisses it accordingly. To such people, belief is completely subjective. The question is not whether it's true but whether it works for you. That might be a legitimate assumption for other religions and self-help philosophies, but Christianity rests on historical, public claims. These claims are either true or false; they cannot be true for some people and not for others.

2. *Shouldn't we just concentrate on loving Jesus and get on with life?* Imagine that you've just been told you have cancer. You're going to need surgery immediately. As you tell the story to your spouse or friend, you are asked details about the diagnosis, the symptoms, and the cure. You shrug and say, "I'm not sure. I'm not a doctor, so I'll just go with the flow."

Well, what *about* the doctor? What are his or her credentials? Has the surgeon performed this operation before? What's the success rate?

Again you shrug. "Hmmm. I haven't really checked."

Obviously, anyone who loves you is going to press you to take it all a little more seriously and do some homework.

"Look," you reply, "I just have to trust the process and hope that it all turns out all right. Right now it's working for me."

This is an absurd scenario for most of us. We would take our physical health more seriously than this person. But what about our spiritual health? Despite medical advances, one day you and I will die. In comparison with eternity, whatever life span we're given seems pretty brief. The time we have now is for asking the big questions—and finding answers. We all have to grapple with the severity of our spiritual illness and its symptoms. We also need to know the credentials of the God who promises a very specific, if drastic, cure. As we hear the success stories, our faith in him grows. It's not just an act of the will—a subjective leap. It is a reasonable trust backed up by his mighty acts throughout biblical history from Genesis to Revelation. All this requires investigation. That is what theology or doctrine is all about: exploring the most important convictions that shape our outlook, desires, hopes, and lives.

The firewall between faith and reason has to come down. Your heart can only embrace someone you know something about. To avoid dealing with doctrine, some say about Christianity, "It's not a religion; it's a relationship." But if you think about it, our closest relationships are not with people about whom we know little. It is only as we get to know people and they prove their character, love, and care that we grow in our desire for their company. Socrates said, "The unexamined life is not worth living." But it's also true that the unexamined faith is not worth believing.

God is either there or he isn't. But it is absurd to imagine that you conjure up his existence and characteristics by an act of personal choice. If God exists, then he is the author of the story that includes you. The gospel—"good news"—that the Christian faith proclaims is either true or false, but it cannot be walled off into a safe room of cuddly bears and the favorite blanket of childhood. Its validity does not depend on how well it works for you, how it makes your life more meaningful, or how it gives you moral direction and inspirational motivation. Instead the gospel is a very particular claim based upon events that happened in datable history with significance for the entire cosmos.

THE 4 DS

O NE WAY TO SEE how knowing, experiencing, and living are interconnected is to describe each main doctrine of the Christian faith in terms of four Ds: drama, doctrine, doxology, and discipleship. These four Ds will guide our exploration. We'll see how doctrine is generated by God's unfolding drama and transforms our experience as well as our everyday lives.

First, doctrine grows out of the biblical *drama*. God reveals what he is like, not in ivory-tower speculation but down on the ground in real history. One reason why many Christians find the Bible inaccessible is that they have not yet been shown how its various parts fit into an unfolding drama that runs from creation and the fall to exodus and redemption all the way to the new creation. The plot with Christ as the central character ties it all together. Every story in the Bible points not to us and how we can have our best life now, but first to Christ and how everything God orchestrates leads to redemption in him.

Second, the drama yields specific *doctrine*. From the throbbing verbs and adverbs of the drama we are given stable nouns. God himself teaches us that he has *acted* wisely, justly, mercifully, and omnisciently because he *is* wise, just, merciful, and all-knowing. In fact, far from being irrelevant and abstract, it is doctrine that tells us what the drama means for us. From the drama we observe that Christ was crucified and raised (1 Cor 15:1–5). But from the doctrine we learn that he was "delivered over to death *for our sins* and was raised to life *for our justification*" (Rom 4:25; emphasis added). We were sitting in the audience, watching the drama unfold, when the Holy Spirit—the casting director—swept us up onto the stage and into the action. We were once "not a people" and "had not received mercy," but now we are part of God's people, coheirs with Christ of his whole estate and recipients of his grace (1 Pet 2:10).

Third, the doctrines rooted in the drama fill us with thankful hearts—*doxology*, meaning "praise." The drama can be astonishing, but apart from the doctrine it can also remain remote. Events happened in history that were beyond our greatest expectations, but what does that mean for us? When God writes us into the script by interpreting what it means for us, we are not just astonished; we are overwhelmed with gratitude. The drama and doctrine are true regardless of our response. However, in worship we internalize the drama. Everything that happened outside of us in history now becomes our story. In worship we are given our own lines in the script, joining the cast of characters. It is not just a great story with interesting doctrines; it grabs our heart.

Fourth, doxology yields the fruit of love and good works—*discipleship*. We are turned outside of ourselves, looking up to God in faith and out to our neighbors in love. We are no longer the central character in our own life movie. Instead, we have been baptized, buried, and raised with Christ. Our dead-end character dies and we're finally part of a drama that is true, good, and beautiful. Living in this drama, informed by the doctrine, and shaped by the experience of true worship, we are able to live out our part in the story wherever God has placed us.

You can see this actually play out in the Psalms—the Bible's hymnal. These songs are rooted in the historical drama of God's faithfulness in spite of his unfaithful people. It is not a catalogue of doctrines. But the doctrines are obvious enough from the drama: the acts of God that define who he is, who we are, and why we should trust him. Though they are basically sung prayers, they are not just a string of emotional self-expression. The psalmist does not repeat, "We worship you," over and over again. Rather, the laments, praise, wonder, and worship are all tied to God's works (the drama) as he interprets them (the doctrine). And they lead to a new way of living in the world.

You can also see this pattern in Paul's letter to the Romans. It begins with the drama, "the gospel of God—the gospel he promised beforehand through his prophets in the Holy Scriptures regarding his Son, who as to his earthly life was a descendant of David, and who through the Spirit of holiness was appointed the Son of God in power by his resurrection from the dead: Jesus Christ our Lord" (Rom 1:1–4).

Then the apostle lays out the doctrinal argument for the whole world being condemned by God's law and yet justified freely by his grace through faith in Christ (1:5–8:30). In this doctrinal section, he unpacks the meaning of the gospel—what God has done for us in Christ, from election to the cross and from there to the Spirit's gift of faith, justification, sanctification, and glorification.

From this alpine summit he exclaims, "What, then, shall we say in response to these things? If God is for us, who can be against us?" (8:31). Absolutely nothing in all creation "will be able to separate us from the love of God that is in Christ Jesus our Lord" (8:39). He's not just explaining the doctrine; he's singing it! After explaining God's plan still further, he again exalts:

> *Oh, the depth of the riches of the wisdom and knowledge of God!*
> *How unsearchable his judgments,*
> *and his paths beyond tracing out!*
> *"Who has known the mind of the Lord?*

> Or who has been his counselor?"
> "Who has ever given to God,
>   that God should repay them?"
> For from him and through him and for him are all things.
>   To him be the glory forever! Amen. (11:33–36)

Amen, indeed!

Finally, Paul turns to the form of discipleship that this should take: "I urge you, brothers and sisters, in view of God's mercy, to offer your bodies as a living sacrifice" (12:1). This is "our reasonable service" when we consider everything he has done for us. No longer living in conformity to the world, we are being transformed by the renewing of our mind through God's Word (12:2).

Every worldview follows something like these four Ds. Marxism and Democracy as well as Hindu, Buddhist, Islamic, and Jewish cultures are each generated by a particular story about the world and become the lens through which people interpret and live out their lives. Such stories have moved armies. Stories are powerful. Where did we come from, who are we, and where are we going? Who can deny that these are the big questions that somehow we've been wired to ask? And the answers drive whole civilizations.

So if we're Christians we need to know the story and its meaning for us. We need to internalize it, responding appropriately to the God who acts. And then we need to be increasingly conformed to the central character as we live as his free people in service to others. In other words we need to engage in theology, which is the study of God. If we are interested in God, we should be interested in theology. Biblical doctrine is not just a head trip. It is an unfolding story in which God invites us to play the part that he created for us from before the foundation of the world (Eph 2:10). Far from a distraction, to know what you believe and why lies at the heart of your Christian experience, worship, and everyday living.

Furthermore, faith is not a subjective leap; it is a reasoned trust in the God who reveals himself clearly in the gospel. The whole Christian faith rests not on our collective feelings, experiences, or moral sentiments but on the public announcement that God has acted in history to save us from sin and death. We now turn to focus on that central claim.

CHAPTER 1

JESUS IS GOD

WATCHING FROM A PARK BENCH as the morning sun gradually swallowed the horizon, I was joined by a young woman. After a bit of small talk, she began to relate challenges that had brought her to question the meaning of life. "Would it make a difference," I asked, "if God had become one of us—not only experiencing our pain but dying and rising again as the start of a new creation?"

"You mean Jesus?" she replied. "I think he was a great man. Probably if everyone lived like he did, the world would be a better place."

A lot of people share her view of Jesus—that he was a great man but not the eternal Son of God who became human for our salvation. Adherents of other religions respect Jesus of Nazareth. Even most atheists I've met express a high regard for the moral principles Jesus taught. But a man—even a great man—could not impart to us joy, confidence, and hope. Only Jesus does that.

→ In him there is joy because we finally have a rescuer—a real savior and redeemer. He's not just another let-down but God in the flesh.

→ In him there is confidence because our identity is no longer lodged in what we do, feel, or think but in being united to him.

→ And in him there is hope because he is the "firstfruits" of the new creation. United to him, we cannot fail to share in his resurrection. Only a human being *should* save us, as our representative, but only God *can*. Jesus is both.

THE PROMISED ONE

A LOT OF PEOPLE start with their personal story. When they are asked about the identity of Jesus they answer, "He is my best friend," or "He lives in my heart," or "He has changed my life." These are wonderful truths. But it is history—*his* story—before it is *my* story. What he did for us all two millennia ago in a land far away from most of us is the headline. Jesus is not swept into your story. You are swept into his. When we start with God's big story, the fact that we can actually have a personal relationship with him becomes even more meaningful.

We see so much of God's big story unfolding in the four Gospels—Matthew, Mark, Luke, and John. Each of the Gospels displays its own audience and intent, yet together each is like a part of an orchestra, blending with the other parts in a harmonious witness to Jesus Christ. For John, Jesus is the eternal Son by whom the Father created the world. The emphasis through this Gospel is on Jesus Christ as the "light of the world" (John 8:12). He is also "the Lamb of God, who takes away the sin of the world" (John 1:29). The whole world lies under the shroud of death because of sin. And Jesus has come to bring everlasting life not only to Jews but to Gentiles (the rest of the nations).

The other three Gospels draw us in a bit more closely to the specific story of Israel. We find ourselves in an unmistakably Jewish atmosphere, yet this story of Israel encompasses the whole world. In fact, as we read the Gospels, even we who were strangers to the covenants and promises that God made to Israel are brought into the unfolding drama.

The Gospels leave out all sorts of details about Jesus that you would expect in a *People* cover story. We know virtually nothing about his childhood, for example. We don't know his favorite color or flavor of ice cream. And yet the Gospels report the names of Roman rulers like Caesar Augustus, Pilate, Felix, and the Jewish king Agrippa. Even Quirinius governor of Syria makes it into the Christmas story (Luke 2:1–2). These names appear in the accounts because the gospel is tied to datable events.

Luke tells us in his Gospel of a devout elder named Simeon. He was "waiting for the consolation of Israel, and the Holy Spirit was on him" (2:25). Furthermore Luke recounts:

> *Now there was a man in Jerusalem called Simeon, who was righteous and devout. He was waiting for the consolation of Israel, and the Holy Spirit was on him. It had been revealed to him by the Holy Spirit that he would not die before he had seen the Lord's Messiah. Moved by the Spirit, he went into the temple courts. When the parents brought in the child Jesus to do for him what the custom of the Law required, Simeon took him in his arms and praised God, saying:*
>
> *"Sovereign Lord, as you have promised,*
> *   you may now dismiss your servant in peace.*
> *For my eyes have seen your salvation,*
> *   which you have prepared in the sight of all nations:*
> *a light for revelation to the Gentiles,*
> *   and the glory of your people Israel." (2:25–32)*

From Gabriel's announcement to Mary that she would conceive and bear the Son of God to this moment in the temple, the identity of the Christ child was wrapped in the history of Israel. Through the Messiah, Israel would not only be saved but would be the means of salvation to the ends of the earth.

The question raised by the appearance of Jesus is whether he is the fulfillment of history for Israel and the whole world. Is he the promised Messiah? Jews divided over the answer, but only because they shared the same story that gave rise to the question in the first place. This is why there was so much conflict in the aftermath of the claim that Jesus had been raised from the dead. Jews understood what Jesus was saying about who he was and what he had come to accomplish. As a result, some followed whereas others charged him with the capital crime of blasphemy. Ever since, Jesus Christ has been to Jews a "stumbling block" just as Isaiah had prophesied centuries earlier (Isa 8:14).

To non-Jews, the Gentiles, the gospel at first did not even rise to the level of an offense; it was simply "foolishness" (1 Cor 1:23). Jesus was the answer to questions that philosophers were not even asking. The Greek philosophers in Jesus's day were obsessed with the latest ideas about eternal principles and the best path for attaining virtue, happiness, and personal fulfillment. They overlooked the highest wisdom, the divine plan for the salvation not only of Jews but also of Gentiles in Jesus Christ (1 Cor 1:18–24). It is not that the Greeks were expecting too much, but that they were settling for too little—their best life now instead of a new creation.

So when the apostle Paul, trained by the greatest Jewish thinker of his day (Gamaliel II), was asked to speak to the philosophers gathered in Athens's Areopagus, he proclaimed the resurrection of Christ and the last judgment (Acts 17:16–34). There is no way, he said, that Jesus could be absorbed in a pantheon of deities. Israel's bedrock confession was belief in one God. Therefore, Jesus of Nazareth was either God coming to rescue his people or the greatest threat yet to have befallen the people of Israel. The one *impossible* option was to say that he was a great man who nevertheless was not who he claimed to be.

THE CASE FOR CHRIST

J ESUS IS GOD. We know this because of the clear claims he made concerning himself and the fact that he rose from the dead just as he promised. Knowing that Christianity stands or falls with this claim, skeptics have focused all their critical energies on this target. So what is the case, after so many centuries of attack?

1. JESUS SAID HE WAS GOD

It is a fact that Jesus claimed he was God. Liberal scholars have attempted for a few centuries now to disprove this claim, following a course similar to Thomas Jefferson, principal author of America's Declaration of Independence. Jefferson famously took scissors to the Bible. Whatever fit with what he believed to be universally known by natural reason he passed over, but passages that reported miracles—especially the incarnation, signs, atoning death, and resurrection of Christ—were excised. Liberal scholars have followed a similar course. Though made with more technical sophistication, their conclusions have been no less arbitrary and controlled by their own anti-supernatural prejudices.

In all the Gospels, Jesus claims for himself equality with God. He performs works that are attributable only to God. He claims to be David's Lord (Matt 22:43–46). He arouses the ire of the religious leaders by forgiving sins, bypassing the temple and its ritual sacrifices. "Who is this who even forgives sins?" they demand (Luke 7:49; cf. Matt 9:6). "Why does this fellow talk like that? He's blaspheming! Who can forgive sins but God alone?" (Mark 2:7). In fact, Jesus claims to be "greater than the temple" and even "Lord of the Sabbath" (Matt 12:6, 8; Luke 6:5).

Jesus appropriates the attributes and actions reserved for God alone, including the personal name Yahweh, or I AM (John 1:1; 8:58). In what is called the "Upper Room Discourse" (John 14–16), Jesus reveals the intimate relationship he shares with the Father and the Spirit—a relationship that began before creation. Then in his prayer in John 17, Jesus speaks of "the glory I had with you before the world began" (v. 5). Additionally, Jesus welcomes Thomas's confession, "My Lord and my God!" (John 20:28–29).

The apostles clearly proclaimed Christ as Yahweh—Israel's God. Paul says that Jesus has been given "the name that is above every name, that at the name of Jesus every knee should bow, in heaven and on earth and under the earth, and every tongue acknowledge that Jesus Christ is Lord, to the glory of God the Father" (Phil 2:9b–11). Paul's words there echo an Old Testament prophecy about Yahweh's sovereign lordship (Isa 45:23). Elsewhere Paul recalls when the Israelites had put Yahweh to the test in the wilderness centuries before and he identifies the offended party in that incident as Christ (1 Cor 10:9). Paul also writes, "God was pleased to have all his fullness dwell in him" (Col 1:19) and he links the "day of the Lord" with Christ's return (1 Thess 5:2). In the book of Revelation, Jesus is "the Alpha and the Omega . . . who is, and who was, and who is to come, the Almighty" (1:8). He is "the First and the Last" and "the Living One" who holds "the keys of death and Hades" (1:17–18).

Some say that Jesus never claimed to be the eternal Son of God, but if that were true, then why was he tried by the highest Jewish court on the charge of blasphemy—specifically because "he was even calling God his own Father, making himself equal with God" (John 5:18)? There is no instance in which Jesus is said to have rejected this charge. And in that same passage he adds:

> *The Father judges no one, but has entrusted all judgment to the Son, that all may honor the Son just as they honor the Father. Whoever does not honor the Son does not honor the Father, who sent him. Very truly I tell you, whoever hears my word and believes him who sent me has eternal life and will not be judged but has crossed over from death to life.* (5:22–24)

"Yes," critics retort, "but how do we know that Jesus actually said these things?" There is an easy answer: *Whatever Jesus said about himself must have been sufficiently provocative to have led the religious leaders to call for capital punishment—on the charge of blasphemy.* It is out of the question that Jewish leaders would have been aroused to commit a respected rabbi to capital punishment for teaching the ethical commands that lay at the heart of their own noble religion. Jesus did not add any new commands to the moral law and when anyone asked what the law required, he simply quoted the Ten Commandments (Luke 18:18–20; see Matt 5:17–20).

In short, the Jesus admired by liberals and skeptics would never have been convicted of blasphemy and crucified. More than anyone, including the religious leaders, he loved Israel's God and his law. Already then, we are faced with the choice that C. S. Lewis suggested over a half century ago that either Jesus is Lord or he was a lunatic:

> *I am trying here to prevent anyone saying the really foolish thing that people often say about Him: I'm ready to accept Jesus as a great moral teacher, but I don't accept his claim to be God. . . . You*

can shut him up for a fool, you can spit at him and kill him as a
demon or you can fall at his feet and call him Lord and God, but
let us not come with any patronising nonsense about his being a
great human teacher. He has not left that open to us. He did not
intend to. . . . . Now it seems to me obvious that He was neither a
lunatic nor a fiend: and consequently, however strange or terrifying
or unlikely it may seem, I have to accept the view that He was and
is God.[1]

Who did Jesus think he was? Any answer we give has to explain his being
sentenced to death for blasphemy.

2. JESUS DIED

It is beyond controversy that Jesus died. The Jews knew that Jesus had
died. In fact, they knew that he was crucified under Pontius Pilate, since
Jewish sources name the Roman prefect. (So much for the Qur'an's
statement made six centuries later far from the epicenter that Jesus only
"made it look as if he died.") Romans were very successful at crucifix-
ions, and there is no record of anyone escaping from their crosses. Even
the liberal New Testament scholar John A. T. Robinson concludes that
Jesus's death and burial in the tomb is "one of the earliest and best-
attested facts about Jesus."[2]

The burial of Jesus in the tomb of Joseph of Arimathea is mentioned
in all four Gospels (Matt 27:57–60; Mark 15:43–46; Luke 23:50–53;
John 19:38–42). This is a specific detail that lends credibility to the
account. Further, it is an embarrassing detail for the disciples since according to their own report (as well as the Jewish Talmud) they fled
the scene, while this high-standing Jewish leader received permission
from Pilate to bury Jesus in his own tomb. Jesus would not have been
handed over to just anyone. Yet the standing of Joseph of Arimathea

was sufficient for Pilate to hand over his body after confirming with the centurion that Jesus was in fact dead (Mark 15:44–45). This confirmation was given after the soldier drove a spear through Jesus's side. Adding to the embarrassment, yet another Jewish leader named Nicodemus assisted in this burial (John 19:38–42). Therefore we can eliminate any theories that leave Jesus only half dead and nursed back to health. Jesus died and was buried.

3. THE TOMB WAS EMPTY AFTER THREE DAYS

Not even this is a controversial claim. According to Matthew 28:11–15, the Jewish leaders maintained that the body was stolen by the disciples. Such a claim proves that everyone believed that the tomb was empty. Romans also expressed alarm at the disruption caused by Jesus's empty tomb. Dated around AD 41, a marble plaque was discovered with an edict of Caesar upon it that commanded capital punishment for anyone who dared to "break a tomb."

4. THE TOMB WAS EMPTY BECAUSE JESUS HAD BEEN RAISED, JUST AS HE HAD PROMISED

Of course, this is where the paths diverge. Josephus (AD 37–100), a Jewish historian from Jerusalem, offers crucial insight outside of the New Testament itself. His writings contain this account:

> At this time there was a wise man called Jesus, and his conduct was good, and he was known to be virtuous. Many people among the Jews and the other nations became his disciples. Pilate condemned him to be crucified and to die. But those who had become his disciples did not abandon his discipleship. They reported that he had appeared to them three days after his crucifixion and that he was alive. Accordingly, he was perhaps the Messiah, concerning

whom the prophets have reported wonders. And the tribe of the Christians, so named after him, has not disappeared to this day.[3]

Everything in Josephus's account is well attested in Jewish sources. The liberal rabbi Samuel Sandmel notes that some Jews believed Jesus was "the long-awaited messiah" and he writes, "After his death, his disciples believed that he was resurrected, and had gone to heaven, but would return to earth at the appointed time for the final divine judgment."[4] Although Rabbi Sandmel himself does not believe these claims, the fact that Jesus's own followers did believe them dispels any notion that they were later inventions of an imaginative church. By the time of a famous letter to Emperor Trajan around AD 110 from Pliny the Younger (governor of what is now Turkey), Christians were reportedly gathering regularly on Sunday to worship Jesus as God (*Epistles* 10.96).

Additionally, there are features of the resurrection reports that lend them credibility. For one, the testimony of women was not admitted into Jewish or Roman courts. Yet it is women who first saw and reported Christ's resurrection. If the disciples had wanted to invent a religion, they surely would have made men, especially themselves, the first witnesses. They surely would not have represented themselves as cowards, still less as those who at first did not believe the women's report. Moreover, whatever happened was enough to transform the disciples into messengers of the risen Jesus. The Peter who denied Jesus three times was later found preaching Christ boldly in Jerusalem itself during a national holiday (Acts 2:14–41). There are many people even today who are willing to die for what they believe in. But do thousands of people die for something that they *know* to be a lie?

It is true that the resurrection is unusual. We do not experience people rising from the dead. Not even Jesus's raising of Lazarus was the same as his own. Lazarus, for example, would go on living—perhaps for many years. But he would eventually succumb once more to death. Only this time it would be after Christ's resurrection. Jesus's friend would die this time in the assurance of rising again one day in the new creation to live forever with Christ.

If Jesus did rise, then its meaning is exactly what he and his disciples said it was: the beginning of the new creation and immortal life defined by the age to come. By definition, what brought about the end of the old age and the beginning of the new is unique. However, to decide in advance what can or cannot happen based on what normally occurs is to put philosophical prejudices before historical investigation. We can remain aloof to the resurrection claim with the assertion that "it cannot happen." But the real question is whether in fact it did happen, regardless of whether we think it could.

Eyewitness testimony is sufficient for our belief today. Critics often say that such testimony is mere hearsay: "If *I* had seen the risen Jesus with my own eyes, I would believe, but how can I believe based on ancient reports?" But this is simply to reject the possibility of doing history at all. Historians are always relying on reports rather than on firsthand observation of the events. By definition, historical sources lie in the past! But to reject the gospel simply because of this fact is an arbitrary act of the will and not an honest investigation.

The case for the risen Christ has enormous implications. If Jesus is raised, then he is the eternal Son of God into whose hands the last judgment has been committed. This was Paul's concluding point in the philosophers' arena of Athens: "In the past God overlooked such ignorance, but now he commands all people everywhere to repent. For he has set a day when he will judge the world with justice by the man he has appointed. He has given proof of this to everyone by raising him from the dead" (Acts 17:30–31).

There is no consolation prize for believers if Christ is not the risen Lord. As Paul also said in 1 Corinthians 15, "And if Christ has not been raised, our preaching is useless and so is your faith. More than that, we are then found to be false witnesses about God, for we have testified about God that he raised Christ from the dead. . . . And if Christ has not been raised, your faith is futile; you are still in your sins. Then those also who have fallen asleep in Christ are lost" (vv. 14–18). But even if it turns out that Jesus was not raised, haven't we lived a happier and more fulfilling life? Paul answers, "If only for this life we have hope in Christ, we are of all people most to be pitied" (v. 19).

To dismiss the Christian claim with a shrug is intellectually irresponsible as well as personally catastrophic. The gospel is not a philosophy that might be true regardless of whether Jesus rose from the dead. It's not a useful therapy for those who need a bit of inspiration and moral direction in a crazy world. In short, Paul says that religion is a waste of time if Jesus is not raised. "If the dead are not raised, 'Let us eat and drink, for tomorrow we die'" (v. 32). The options are stark. Jesus is either the *Lord*, or he is a *liar* or *lunatic*.

FROM DRAMA TO DOCTRINE: WHAT CHRISTIANS BELIEVE ABOUT JESUS AS GOD

S O FAR I HAVE OFFERED a defense of the Christian claim that Jesus is God. The drama gives rise to particular doctrines that we find in the teaching of the apostles. Jesus did not become God. Rather God the Son—the second person of the Trinity—assumed our humanity without laying aside his deity. This is called the *hypostatic union*, meaning that there is *one person*, Jesus Christ, in *two natures* (divine and human). Without this doctrine Christianity would be like other religions—nothing more than a system of morals, symbols, and rituals.

Not everyone agrees, though. There have always been people—even pastors and leaders—who question this consensus.

First were the Ebionites, who considered Jesus the greatest prophet but not God incarnate. Later the *Arians* taught that Jesus was merely the first and most preeminent creature. While these heresies rejected Christ's deity, *Docetism* denied his full humanity—Jesus merely appeared to be human.

Other heresies arose over the union of the two natures (divine and human) in Christ. At one end, *Nestorianism*

HYPOSTATIC UNION

A theological term used in the early church to describe the union of the divine and human natures in the one person of Jesus Christ (*hypostasis* = underlying state or reality).

separated the two natures to the point of rendering them two *persons*. At the opposite end, Monophysitism (one-nature-ism) collapsed Christ's humanity into his deity. The Council of Chalcedon (AD 451) settled this dispute: Jesus Christ is one person in two natures. His divine and human natures are neither to be separated nor confused.

From different directions all these heresies rejected the gospel's central message: that *God* had become *one of us* to rescue us from sin and death. All these false views of Christ are still evident today. Mormonism teaches that Jesus was the first "spirit child" of the Father rather than the unique Son of God. Jehovah's Witnesses deny his deity, claiming that he is simply the first creature made by God. Many historically Christian churches have been infected by a liberal theology that rejects Christ's uniqueness as the eternally begotten Son of the Father.

ANCIENT HERESIES ABOUT CHRIST

EBIONITES	Jesus was not God, but a superior prophet and moral teacher who guides us to our salvation through obedience to the law.
ARIANISM	The Son is a created being; there was a time when he did not exist.
DOCETISM	Christ only appeared to have a human body.
NESTORIANISM	Separates the two natures of Christ. Nestorians believed that Mary was the mother of Jesus (human nature), but not of God (divine nature).
MONOPHYSITISM	Combines the two natures of Christ. It taught that in the incarnation the two natures became one, with the divine absorbing the human.

"WHO DO *YOU* SAY THAT I AM?"

IN THE MIDDLE of his ministry Jesus asked his disciples, "'Who do people say I am?' They replied, 'Some say John the Baptist; others say Elijah; and still others, one of the prophets'" (Mark 8:27–28). But then he gets a little more personal. "'But what about you?' he asked. 'Who do you say I am?' Peter answered, 'You are the Messiah'" (v. 29).

Scripture not only reveals the *drama* that proves Jesus's claim concerning himself; it interprets the drama in *doctrinal* detail. We now come to know not only who Jesus is but also what it means for us that he is who he said he was and did what he came to accomplish.

What is our response? That is where *doxology* comes into the picture. Jesus is no longer an obscure figure in the distant past, but he confronts us now with the question, "Who do you say that I am?" We can respond with awe and thanksgiving: "My Lord and my God!" (John 20:28). Or we can respond with outrage: "This fellow is blaspheming!" (Matt 9:3). Or we can respond with Pilate's shrug, "What is truth?" (John 18:38).

Those who say with Peter, "You are the Messiah," not only worship but follow. They are *disciples*. They become part of the growing witnesses to Christ and coheirs of the kingdom of God. Swept into God's story, they may not yet know exactly where they're going and what troubles they will meet along the way. But they can say with Paul, "This is no cause for shame, because I know whom I have believed, and am convinced that he is able to guard what I have entrusted to him until that day" (2 Tim 1:12). The rest of our life is a pilgrimage to the city of God.

So Jesus presses you today with the question he asked his disciples. It's the most important question you will ever be asked: "But who do *you* say that I am?"

CHAPTER 2

GOD IS THREE PERSONS

"LORD, I THANK YOU for your love and for dying on the cross to save us and for living in our hearts."

I've heard a lot of prayers like this by Christians who affirm the doctrine of the Trinity. But it is an instance not just of doctrine shaping doxology, but also vice versa. A wise maxim from the Middle Ages says, *lex orandi, lex credendi*, which means "the law of praying is the law of believing." Our prayers, both said and sung, shape our beliefs.

So what is wrong with that prayer? It is wrong because it assumes that God is one person. It fails to follow the grain of the biblical drama in which all good gifts come from the Father, in the Son, by the Spirit. The Father gave his Son, but it is the Son who gave his life for us, and it is the Holy Spirit who indwells us. The three persons are engaged in every work together but differently—according to the unique characteristics of each. Whether in the work of creation, providence, or redemption, the Father is the source, the Son is the mediator, and the Spirit is the one at work within the world—and within us—to bring the work to completion.

So what do you mean when you say, "God"? Do you think, pray, and worship in a Trinitarian way? And what difference does it make anyway? Is the doctrine of the Trinity biblical, much less essential to the Christian faith?

"In the doctrine of the Trinity," wrote Herman Bavinck, "beats the heart of the whole revelation of God for the redemption of humanity." As the Father, the Son, and the Spirit, "our God is above us, before us, and within us."[5] The doctrine of the Trinity—God as one in essence and three in person—shapes and structures all of Christian faith and practice.

With this doctrine it becomes most evident that we do not all worship the same God. On the one hand, Christians affirm *one God*. This distinguishes the Christian faith from all religions that are polytheistic (believing in many gods), pantheistic (believing that everything is divine), or nontheistic (such as Buddhism). On the other hand, Christianity also affirms with equal emphasis that this one God exists in *three persons*: the Father, the Son, and the Holy Spirit. This sets it apart from the major monotheistic religions (Judaism and Islam).

WORLDVIEWS

TRINITARIAN THEISM	One God exists in three persons.
POLYTHEISM	Belief in many gods.
PANTHEISM	All is divine.
NONTHEISTIC/ATHEISTIC	No God, or God does not exist.

Isn't it a contradiction to say that we believe that God is both one and three? It certainly would be if we said that God is both one and three in essence or both one and three in persons. However, Christians confess that God is one in *essence* and three in *persons*. It is certainly a mystery. We will never comprehend how the one God exists in three persons. But it is not a contradiction.

The doctrine of the Trinity arises from the drama and is embedded in the doxology and discipleship of God's people. All the first Christians were Jews and proclaimed the God of their fathers as the only true God, yet they were faced with the unfolding drama of God-made-flesh. Jesus is God, but he distinguished himself from the Father. Then, with the Spirit's descent at Pentecost the followers of Christ were faced with the reality of the third person of the Trinity. During his earthly ministry, Jesus taught that the eternally existing Spirit would be sent from heaven when Jesus ascended. After that event they could reread their own Scriptures (the Old Testament) and see the three persons of the Trinity striding together across history.

A PRIMARY MATTER

IN SHORT, THE DOCTRINE of the Trinity is not a secondary matter. Apart from this doctrine, our redeeming Mediator could not actually save us because he would not be God. And the indwelling Spirit could not give us life and indwell us as God's own resurrection-guaranteeing presence. Apart from the Trinity, the Son and the Spirit would be either different names for the same person or mere creatures, however

exalted. Our salvation hangs in the balance of whether God is the Father, the Son, and the Holy Spirit.

ONE GOD

Over against the polytheistic religions of Israel's neighbors, the first presupposition of the Bible is that there is one God. It's revealed in Israel's creed, the *Shema*: "Hear, O Israel: The Lord our God, the Lord is one." The apostles follow this emphasis. Paul says that while the Gentiles worship many so-called gods, "yet for us there is but one God, the Father, from whom all things came and for whom we live; and there is but one Lord, Jesus Christ, through whom all things came and through whom we live" (1 Cor 8:6). There is "one God" (Eph 4:6). Paul's mission was to turn Gentiles "from idols to serve the living and true God" (1 Thess 1:9), and this was Peter's mission as well (1 Pet 4:3). Before the Roman governor Felix, Paul confessed, "I worship the God of our ancestors as a follower of the Way, which they call a sect. I believe everything that is in accordance with the Law and that is written in the Prophets" (Acts 24:14).

THREE PERSONS

So how did it come to be that these Jewish apostles—and the first Christian communities—began to worship Jesus of Nazareth—and the Holy Spirit—as God? That they did so is an established fact, which we know not only from the biblical sources but also from the description of early Christian worship by non-Christian (both Jewish and Roman) sources.

Since doctrine arises out of the unfolding biblical drama, it is unsurprising that the Trinity is more clearly revealed later in the story in the New Testament. However, when we reread the Old Testament in its light, we pick up on references that we (and old-covenant believers) may easily have overlooked. As early as the first two verses of Genesis, we're told that when the Father spoke the creation into existence, "the Spirit of God was hovering over the waters" (Gen 1:1–2). And at times we see a servant of God such as the "angel of the Lord" identified as God himself (Gen 22:11–18; 32:24–30; Exod 3:2–6). Later, in the Psalms and Prophets the coming Messiah is laureled with attributes that belong to God alone.

The early Christians did not arrive at the doctrine of the Trinity by theological speculation. Like the gospel itself, the New Testament brings to clear expression that revelation of the Trinity that was more obscurely present all along in the Old Testament. Jesus is the Son who existed with the Father before the ages and was made human "when the set time had fully come" (Gal 4:4; cf. Rom 1:1–5). With intentional echoes of Genesis 1, John 1 begins, "In the beginning was the Word, and the Word was with God, and the Word was God. He was with God in the beginning" (vv. 1–2). Here the Son is distinct from the Father. There are two persons, yet the Son is identified as God along with the Father. He is "the one and only Son, who came from the Father" (v. 14) and "is himself God and is in closest relationship with the Father" (v. 18).

Paul follows the same formula. Jesus Christ is "the image of the invisible God. . . . For in him all things were created: things in heaven and on earth, visible and invisible, whether thrones or powers or rulers or authorities; all things have been created through him and for him. He is before all things, and in him all things hold together" (Col 1:15–17).

The Father, the Son, and the Spirit were all involved in creation. Yet each was involved in a different way. We also see the doctrine of the Trinity arising out of the drama of Jesus's baptism (Matt 3:13–17; Mark 1:9–11; Luke 3:21–22; John 1:32–34). In that story we find the Father who speaks ("This is my Son, whom I love"), the beloved Son who is baptized, and the Spirit hovering above Jesus as he did over the waters in creation.

The doctrine arose out of the drama of redemption. God came

down to us, and he was the Son who existed eternally with the Father. Now he is one of us: a human being, though still God. Then there is the Holy Spirit, who not only descended at Jesus's baptism but also at Pentecost. People experienced Jesus as God in his life, death, and resurrection. Then they came to know the Holy Spirit as God when he was poured out at Pentecost. Whatever views you have had of God have to catch up with the story. God is three persons.

DEVELOPMENT OF THE DOCTRINE IN CHURCH HISTORY

SIBLING RIVALRY can be a fairly sordid business, especially when children are close in age. Bitter disputes break out over whose turn it is to walk the dog. The gospel is good news for the whole world, but it was immediately intelligible to a Jewish audience. At least to the extent that a hearer knew the Hebrew scriptures (the Old Testament), the message that Jesus was their fulfillment was fairly straightforward. As we saw in chapter 1, the religious leaders knew exactly what Jesus was claiming about himself and charged him with blasphemy. The earliest followers of Jesus were as Jewish as their enemies. In terms of ethnic identity and religious history, it was a family quarrel. It was a struggle over the identity of God and of Israel.

As Jesus promised, the gospel spread from Jerusalem and Judea to "the ends of the earth" (Acts 1:8). From the Roman perspective, the dispute about Jesus could only be seen at first as an inner-Jewish sibling rivalry—except for the fact that the claim "Jesus is Lord" was an act of treason. Religion and politics were as intertwined in the Roman Empire as they were in Israel. At minimum one had to affirm the divinity of the Caesar, and the titles "Savior" and "Lord" belonged to him alone.

Besides the thorny political issue, the spread of the gospel in the empire encountered philosophical roadblocks. The different reactions are interesting. The apostle Paul said that Jews typically regarded the gospel as "a stumbling block" and an offense, while Greco-Roman audiences tended to consider it "foolishness." "Jews demand signs and Greeks seek for wisdom" (see 1 Cor 1:21–23). Philosophy is the "love of wisdom." Truth was considered timelessly eternal. So the idea that the most important truths of all were actually historical events made little sense. Beyond this the gospel made little sense in this Gentile worldview. For the dominant philosophical schools of thought, the soul was the immortal and divine part of a person, and the best thing that could happen to a soul is to be freed from its bodily prison. So how can the resurrection of the body be good, much less liberating? The point of life is to contemplate eternal truth and follow the precepts of nature. Each school had its own program, but for the most part they agreed that the goal of philosophy was happiness.

Some liberal scholars have argued that belief in Jesus's deity with the doctrine of the Trinity as its logical conclusion was the result of Greco-Roman influences. The implausibility of this idea is increasingly recognized. On the contrary, belief in the Trinity arose from the drama—the events that unfolded not in Athens or Rome centuries later—but in Jerusalem in the wake of Christ's resurrection.

Then there was Pentecost where the Spirit was poured out on the church just as the prophets foretold. In fact, at Jesus's baptism there were three divine persons: the Father whose voice was heard, the Spirit who descended in the form of a dove, and Jesus of whom the Father said, "This is my Son, whom I love; with him I am well pleased" (Matt 3:17). In his Great Commission, Jesus told his disciples to baptize "in the name of the Father and of the Son and of the Holy Spirit" (Matt 28:19). Jews knew precisely what it meant to be baptized "in the name of" someone. There is only one God, one name. Jesus's command entails nothing less than that this one God exists in three persons.

But as Christianity gained converts and critics among cultural elites in the Roman world, it had more philosophical challenges to face. The worship of the old gods (polytheism) still had some hold on the populace. However, philosophers were more skeptical. Roughly four centuries before Christ, Plato and Aristotle had argued that all of reality can be traced to a single source, "the One." As the sun emanates light by its rays, it was thought that the One emanates "being." That which is closest to the "sun" obviously has more light (or being). This would include spiritual entities. Flowing down the scale of being, you pass the natures that are pure spirit to those that have bodies. Matter is at the low end of the scale. There were different philosophical schools in the first century but this one, called Platonism, was a major influence. The basic problem then was this: How could God be "the One" and yet "three"?

ANCIENT HERESIES ABOUT GOD

ORIGEN	SUBORDINATIONISM	The Father is the One; Son and Spirit are less "divine."
ARIUS	ARIANISM	Only the Father is God; the Son is created.
SABELLIUS	MODALISM	Father, Son, and Spirit are "masks" of one divine person.

One way of solving this problem was to say that the Father is "the One" in the highest sense. The Son and the Holy Spirit are a little less divine than the Father. Origen of Alexandria (AD 184–253) taught this view. However, it was rejected as the heresy of *subordinationism* since it made the Son and the Spirit subordinate (less than) the Father in divinity.

Later Arius (AD 256–336) went a step further by claiming that Jesus was the first created being and that only the Father is God. "There exists a trinity," he said, "in unequal glories."[6] The Father alone is God, properly speaking, while there was a time when the Son did not exist. *Arianism* became a major challenge to the ancient church. In fact, it spread quickly through ditties that were sung during daily chores. This once again shows the importance of doxology—how we worship and what we sing and pray—for what we believe and how we live. Arianism was firmly rejected by the church but it continued to have dedicated adherents.

Seeking a middle way, *semi-Arianism* argued that the Son is of a *similar*, though not exactly of the same, essence as the Father.

A somewhat different way of preserving the unity of God was struck by the third-century Roman minister Sabellius. He argued that the Father, the Son, and the Spirit are "masks" or personae worn by the one divine person. Like an actor on the stage, God could appear sometimes as the Father, other times as the Son, and other times as the Spirit. These are not in reality three distinct actors, but one person who reveals himself in three modes or masks. That's why this heresy is often called "*modalism.*" Though Sabellius was excommunicated in AD 220, modalism has remained a recurring challenge throughout church history. In fact, it is evident in the prayer I cited at the beginning of this chapter. Even public prayers by ministers are often offered "in your name, amen" as if we were praying to the Father without a mediator!

Many of the analogies people use to "explain" the Trinity lean in a modalistic direction. You may have heard the Trinity likened to a shamrock with different petals or to water as steam, liquid, and ice. One time I heard the Trinity compared to a ceiling fan with different blades! The heresy of modalism might be our default setting. We want to affirm that Jesus is *God*, but we can easily confuse this with saying that he is *the Father.* That's why we need the discipline of Trinitarian prayers and songs in our public and private worship, like: "Glory be to the Father and to the Son and to the Holy Spirit, one God forever. Amen."

Any statement of the relationship of the Son and the Spirit to the Father has to fit with the clear statements of Scripture:

→ God is one. Therefore, the heresy of *tritheism* is ruled out. The three persons are not three Gods.

→ However, the Son is God and the Holy Spirit is God. Scripture does not allow the option of "sort-of-divine-but-not-quite." So *Arianism* and *semi-Arianism* cannot work.

→ At the same time, the Father, the Son, and the Spirit are three distinct persons, not just different roles played by one person. If God were only one person, then what about Jesus's baptism? In that scene, you have three distinct actors: the Father who speaks, the Son who is baptized, and the Spirit who descends as a dove. So *modalism* is out of the question.

In our day these ancient heresies are embraced by Jehovah's Witnesses (Arianism), Latter-Day Saints or Mormons (polytheism), and by liberal theologies who tend toward Arian, semi-Arian, or modalistic views.

To cut the story short, the church fathers gathered at Nicaea in AD 325 to hammer out a clear confession of the faith that was already being preached and practiced in all orthodox churches. Even if everyone agreed on the substance of the doctrine taught in Scripture, how do you *say* it? You want to affirm that the Son and the Spirit are *God* in the same way as the Father ("of the same essence") without saying that they are just the *same person* (the modalist heresy). The consensus reached at the Council of Nicaea (receiving its final form at the Council of Constantinople in AD 381) remains the church's confession to this day.

So the *essence* is one. The persons are *God* in exactly the same way and to exactly the same degree. They are equally omniscient, omnipotent, eternal, loving, just, and holy. The Son and the Spirit are therefore

THE NICENE CREED

A doctrinal statement that is the result of the first ecumenical (universal) church council in AD 325, revised to its final form in AD 381 at the Council of Constantinople. The creed affirms that the Son and the Spirit are of the same essence as the Father, but are each different persons.

> We believe in one God,
> the Father, the Almighty,
> maker of heaven and earth,
> of all that is, seen and unseen.
> We believe in one Lord, Jesus Christ,
> the only son of God,
> eternally begotten of the Father,
> God from God, Light from Light,
> true God from true God,
> begotten, not made,
> of one being with the Father.
> Through him all things were made.
> For us and for our salvation
> he came down from heaven:
> by the power of the Holy Spirit
> he became incarnate from the Virgin Mary,
> and was made man.
> For our sake he was crucified under Pontius Pilate;
> he suffered death and was buried.
> On the third day he rose again
> in accordance with the Scriptures;
> he ascended into heaven
> and is seated at the right hand of the Father.
> He will come again in glory
> to judge the living and the dead,
> and his kingdom will have no end.
> We believe in the Holy Spirit, the Lord, the giver of life,
> who proceeds from the Father [and the Son].
> With the Father and the Son
> he is worshipped and glorified.
> He has spoken through the Prophets.
> We believe in one holy catholic and apostolic Church.
> We acknowledge one baptism for the forgiveness of sins.
> We look for the resurrection of the dead,
> and the life of the world to come. AMEN.

of the same essence (*homoousios*). But the *persons* are three. Each has his own personal attributes that distinguish him from the others. The Father is the unbegotten source of all things, the Son is the only-begotten Son, and the Spirit proceeds from the Father and the Son. The Father gave his Son, and the Spirit unites us to him.

PERICHORESIS

A term first used by the Cappadocian fathers, referring to the mutual indwelling and fellowship of the persons of the Trinity.

Thus, unity and plurality receive equal appreciation: "No sooner do I conceive of the One," said Gregory of Nazianzus, "than I am illumined by the Splendor of the Three; no sooner do I distinguish Them than I am carried back to the One."[7]

Theologians describe the interrelationship between the persons of the Trinity with the term *perichoresis*, which refers to the mutual indwelling of the persons in each other. This is underscored in John's Gospel, where the Son is depicted as in closest relationship with his Father (1:18). No one comes to the Father except through the Son; in fact, to know the Son is to know the Father also (14:6–7). "Don't you believe that I am in the Father, and that the Father is in me?" (v. 10).

THE DIFFERENCE IT MAKES

FROM THE DRAMA and the doctrine, there are the doxologies. Some of the most foundational passages for faith in the Trinity come from expressions of praise in the church's worship. Confessing that God is "one God in three persons" arises naturally from the formulas we find in the New Testament, especially in the context of baptism, blessings, and benedictions (Matt 28:19; John 1:18; 5:23; Rom 5:5–8; 1 Cor 6:11; 8:6; 12:4–6; 2 Cor 13:13–14; Eph 4:4–6; 2 Thess 2:13; 1 Tim 2:5; 1 Pet 1:2). The Father is worshiped as God. The Son is worshiped as God. The Holy Spirit is worshiped as God. And yet there is one God. God the Father is now "our Father" in Jesus Christ. The relationship that the incarnate Son has with the Father by nature is now ours by adoption. Jesus Christ is God but is different from the Father. The Holy Spirit is also God, but is neither the Father nor the Son. This is not the fruit of ivory-tower speculation or of religious imagination. The facts of history forced the first Christians to think about God and worship God and follow God in a way that they never could have invented for themselves.

So the church's teaching on the Trinity emerges from the drama, the doctrine, and the doxology of Scripture. Yet it also arises from the discipleship prescribed and practiced in the apostolic community.

The father of liberal Protestantism Friedrich Schleiermacher dismissed the Trinity as nonessential because he said it makes no difference to religious experience and living. Since we only experience "God" and not "three persons," why should it matter? However, Schleiermacher's approach is deeply flawed because it is based on our pious experience rather than on external revelation. Moreover, he missed one of the most intriguing features that gave rise to belief in the Trinity in the first place, namely, that people did in fact experience the Father, the Son, and the Spirit as distinct yet divine persons. They encountered the incarnate Son (1 John 1:1–4). They experienced the Spirit as he descended at Pentecost and indwelled believers. Not even in terms of personal experience, then, can one regard the Trinity as nonessential.[8]

Far from renouncing the God of Israel, the earliest Christians believed that they were worshiping the God of their fathers and mothers. Yet there they were, faced with Jesus as God the Son in human flesh and God the Spirit descending and indwelling. There they were, being baptized—at Christ's behest—in the name of the Father, the Son, and the Holy Spirit, and being blessed with Trinitarian benedictions.

We experience this wonderful truth in the salvation that comes to us from the Father, in the Son, and through the Spirit. All three persons are dedicated to our salvation, working in distinct ways toward the completion of a single work of redemption. The Father is the source of this redemption. And yet the one who saved us is none other than God the Son. The one who indwells us even now is not a creature or a majestic angel but God the Spirit.

The Trinity is not just an orthodox dogma to which we yield our assent. Placing our trust in Christ, the eternal Son by nature, we are made children by adoption. His Father becomes our Father. And we can only do this because of the gift of faith granted to us by the Holy Spirit, who unites us to Christ. We worship, pray, confess, and sing our laments and praises to the Father, in the Son, by the Spirit. We are baptized and blessed in the name of the Father, and the Son, and the Holy Spirit.

From this lively eternal fellowship of the three persons of the Godhead, there arises a world and a church of diversity and mutual delight. Paul's doxology in Romans 11:36—"From him and through him and for him are all things"—now means more than one divine person being the source, effectual agent, and end of all things. It means that all good gifts come from the Father, through the Spirit, and to the Son. No less than the Father are the Son and the Spirit our creator and preserver. No less than the Son are the Father and the Spirit our Savior and Lord. No less than the Father and the Son is the Spirit worshiped and glorified.

CHAPTER 3

GOD IS GREAT AND GOOD

EVERY NOW AND AGAIN, news reports flash images of Islamic protesters chanting in Arabic, "God is great!" The late Christopher Hitchens, an outspoken atheist writer, countered with his book *God Is Not Great*. Given the horrendous evils in the world, many people who profess to believe in God assume that a choice has to be made. God cannot be both good and great. If he is good, then he is not great enough to stop tsunamis and terrorists. If he is great, then he is not good or doesn't care enough to keep terrible things from happening.

Christians celebrate God's greatness but they also revel in his goodness. The simple child's prayer over meals has it right: "God is great, God is good; let us thank him for our food. Amen." A God who is great but not good is an all-powerful monster. Yet a God who is good but not great cannot save us.

At the outset we need to be humble in approaching the knowledge of God. We don't find God; he finds us. We do not know God the way he knows himself. His mysterious being transcends all that we can ever know. His greatness is like a majestic mountain peak whose summit is hidden in the clouds. God alone is "the blessed and only Ruler, the King of kings and Lord of lords, who alone is immortal and who lives in unapproachable light, whom no one has seen or can see. To him be honor and might forever. Amen" (1 Tim 6:15–16).

And yet we do know what God is like to the extent that he has graciously revealed himself. That is why we talk about God's *attributes*, characteristics he has disclosed to us in his Word. In the drama of creation, redemption, and consummation, God acts consistently in certain ways that identify his character.

We need to keep in mind that from this drama we get the doctrines that fill us with praise (doxology) and shape our lives (discipleship). This chapter explores the character of God as we discover it in the unfolding drama of Scripture.

GOD IS GREAT

YOU MAY HAVE SEEN the poster that reads, "Two Basic Facts: There Is a God and You Are Not He." We tend to imagine God as someone like us only bigger, smarter, and more powerful. However, God is not just more than we are. He is in a class all by himself. He alone is eternal, immortal, all-powerful, all-wise, and all-knowing. His majesty is beyond our power to comprehend.

GOD'S GREATNESS

ASEITY	God is self-existent and independent from creatures.
UNITY (OR SIMPLICITY)	God is not made up of different parts; he is undivided. His attributes are identical with his being.
IMMUTABILITY	God is unchanging.
ETERNITY	God transcends our categories of time, space, and freedom. He is omniscient, omnipresent, and omnipotent.

SELF-EXISTENT (ASEITY)

First, God is great because he is independent of the world. The technical term for this attribute is *aseity*, literally, "from-himselfness." Sometimes it is said that God created the world because he was lonely and wanted fellowship. This cannot be true. After all, God is triune. Three divine persons loving and enjoying each other hardly fit with the picture of a lonely deity wringing his hands until we came along. Add to that the myriad assembly of angelic hosts.

God created a universe that he did not need. Thus creation was founded in freedom and love. But God's independence from the world does not imply that he is disinterested. He is not sitting in Buddha-like detachment, contemplating his inner majesty. On the contrary, he wants to give us life and bring us into a relationship with himself—out of love, not necessity.

SIMPLE (UNITY) AND UNCHANGING (IMMUTABLE)

Second, God is pure spirit, as Jesus told us (John 4:24). Unlike us, he is not made up of parts, passions, and potentialities. God is simple and unified, meaning that his attributes are not literally different aspects of God's essence, but various descriptions of God's unified being. God is also incapable of change—or, to use the technical term, he is *immutable*. We and everything we know in creation are subject to mutation, but God never changes.

We can change for better or worse, but for a perfect God change could mean only corruption. We are constantly growing, realizing our potential. But God has no potential to realize. He is eternally everything that he has always been and will always be. He is not only immutable in his being but also in his perfect plan and purpose. Nowhere is this made clearer than in the crucifixion of Jesus, who, we are told, was "handed over . . . by God's deliberate plan and foreknowledge" (Acts 2:23). He has a perfect plan and purpose for each one of us also, as we learn from the psalmist:

> *Your eyes saw my unformed body;*
> *   all the days ordained for me were*
> *written in your book*
> *   before one of them came to be. (Ps 139:16)*

God remains faithful to his everlasting purposes regardless of the opposition and obstacles that we place in his path.

To be sure, the Bible represents God as changing his intentions. For example, he warns his people that he will judge them if they violate his command, and yet he "relents" and does not bring disaster upon them (e.g., Jer 18:7–10; Joel 2:12–13). However, what changes is not God's *eternal* purpose secret to us, but the terms of his *revealed* will.

In other words, whatever God does he has determined to do all along. God shows compassion, love, anger, and other emotions. However, he is never caught by surprise or overwhelmed because he knows all things from eternity and has already figured our free actions into his secret plan.

OMNISCIENT

Third, God is *omniscient*. He knows the end from the beginning because he is *eternal*. We are creatures of time. Therefore, we know things in serial fashion: first this, then that. We may guess about what will happen in the future, but God transcends our limited perspective. For him everything in time is already part of his eternal plan. This is comforting. We could hardly trust God's victory over evil, sin, and death if his judgments and actions were based on guesswork.

OMNIPRESENT

Fourth, God is *omnipresent*. This too is an implication of the fact that he is eternal and pure spirit. It is not just that he is in many places at once or even that he is everywhere at once. Rather, it is that God transcends the whole category of "place." Yet this does not mean that God is nowhere. On the contrary, he can freely enter into all of our places and times as he pleases. Even when he is pleased to identify his special presence in a particular place, like the temple in Jerusalem, it is for our benefit rather than his. As creatures not only of time but also of space, we could not experience his presence apart from particular places. The key is to find him where he has promised to find us: in the places that he specifically identifies as the site of his presence in blessing rather than judgment.

OMNIPOTENT

Fifth, God is *omnipotent*, that is, all-powerful. Sometimes we talk about God's sovereignty and human freedom as if they were pieces of a pie. God may have a larger piece, but it's the same pie. Or we think in terms of a seesaw: to the extent that God is sovereign, we have less freedom and responsibility. Both these images misunderstand a crucial point. God is not just quantitatively greater than us; he is qualitatively different. God has 100 percent of the kind of freedom that only he can have as the eternal God, while we have 100 percent of the kind of freedom that is appropriate to creatures.

God made us in his image, yet only Jesus is his eternal Son by nature. We are children of God by gracious adoption. That means that we are like God in a sense: he has freedom and has given us freedom. Yet God has the kind of freedom that only an unchangeable, eternal, omniscient, and omnipotent God can have. Our kind of freedom is different. God created human beings with real power to decide and act, yet God's eternal plan governs everything that happens including our free acts. Scripture clearly teaches both truths: God's sovereignty and human responsibility. But we are not told how they can both be true. Like the Trinity, there is mystery here without contradiction.

GOD IS GOOD

G OD IS GREAT but he is also good. He reigns in majesty beyond anything that we can understand or experience, but he also stoops to our level to reveal himself and to deliver his saving gifts. To say that God is good is to affirm his love, compassion, faithfulness, justice, righteousness, holiness, and jealousy.

GOD'S GOODNESS

LOVE	Favor toward and regard for the other.
COMPASSION/MERCY	God's favor toward those who deserve his wrath.
JUSTICE	An absolute commitment to do what is right and true and to judge transgressors.
RIGHTEOUSNESS	Similar to justice; God's integrity. His inability to sin.
HOLINESS	Separate from all unrighteousness and injustice; God's unique ethical purity.
JEALOUSY	God's love for his people that binds them to him against slavery to other lords.
FAITHFULNESS	God does not change and always keeps his promises.

LOVING, COMPASSIONATE, MERCIFUL

First, God is *loving, compassionate*, and *merciful*. There is nothing like the biblical story to convince us of these truths. "God is love," John tells us (1 John 4:8). And from the prophet we hear God say, "I take no pleasure in the death of the wicked, but rather that they turn from their ways and live" (Ezek 33:11). It is not surprising that a God who is majestic in glory beyond our grandest thoughts might create a world for his glory. What is more amazing is that he goes on loving the world and us in spite of our sin. God loved us even "while we were God's enemies" (Rom 5:10). Some people are so victimized over the course of many years that their character is shaped by those experiences. They find it hard to love because they have never been loved. But God can love those who show him only hatred and contempt because his love does not depend on what they think, feel, or do. He *is* love.

Compassion is an implication of his love in the face of opposition. Instead of retaliating, God's first thought is to show compassion. He has pity on those who choose to trust in themselves or the things they have made. Yet God doesn't have to show mercy to anyone. In fact God told Moses, "I will have mercy on whom I will have mercy, and I will have compassion on whom I will have compassion" (Exod 33:19; see also Rom 9:15). God has freely chosen to bestow not only his love but also his compassion and mercy on those who deserve the very opposite.

JUST, RIGHTEOUS, HOLY, JEALOUS

Second, God is *just, righteous, holy*, and *jealous*. These attributes underscore God's fidelity to his goodness in a number of ways. God's judgment of sinners throughout the history of the Bible is often viewed as cruel. How could God send Israelites to war to destroy every living person and animal occupying the land of Canaan? This confuses us. We wonder how a good God could do that. But he actually did it *because* he is good. Here were people who for centuries offered up their children as sacrifices to Baal and invaded neighboring countries in violent raids. Moreover, the Canaanites and other nations in the land were idolatrous and immoral. They were also occupying and polluting the land that God had promised to Abraham. The whole earth is the Lord's. So the really amazing thing is that he didn't wipe every one of our ancestors from the face of the earth and start over. Instead, he localized the holy wars to the land that he promised to Abraham. We really do not know how sinful we are. If we did, we would see God's justice, righteousness, and holiness as absolutely essential to his goodness.

FAITHFUL

Third, God is *faithful*. In one sense this draws together many of God's other attributes. He does not change, because he is faithful to himself—his own character being the gold standard of everything great and good—and that is why he judges. He is faithful to his law, his justice, and his holiness. He cannot relax his justice any more than he can limit his power, omniscience, or any other aspect of his deity. But he is faithful also to his *promises*. And he sent his Son to fulfill his law and to bear our curses for having violated it. He provided the only way of his being "just *and* the one who justifies those who have faith in Jesus" (Rom 3:26; emphasis added).

He found the way to be faithful to his promise to save sinners without being unfaithful to himself: he sent his Son. This is our refuge. If God were fickle, as we are, then the slightest defection might provoke the renunciation of his former compassion. He could fly off in a rage. Yet God fulfills his promises. He must. In fact, "if we are faithless, he remains faithful, for he cannot disown himself" (2 Tim 2:13).

IF GOD IS GREAT AND GOOD, HOW CAN THERE BE SO MUCH EVIL IN THE WORLD?

THERE ARE A LOT OF MYSTERIES surrounding the attributes of God. The Bible teaches us both that God is all-powerful and that we have real freedom and responsibility. But *how*? We know from the Bible that God is just and yet also merciful. But *how* can both be true given our sin? Jesus is the answer to the mystery. Yet it still remains mysterious in the sense that we cannot understand exactly how it all works behind the scenes. What God has revealed is nevertheless enough for us to trust his character.

The real test comes when we read the newspaper or experience trag-edies. How can we affirm God's goodness amidst the horrific evils in the world, both natural and moral? Either God is great or God is good, but he can't be both. This is the great problem that Christians have to face.

What is evil? The answer varies, depending on one's view of God and his relation to the world. Again, the doctrines arise out of the drama: the different stories that tell us where we came from, who we are, and where we're going. In a pantheistic worldview where the world is seen as divine, evil is an illusion. In most polytheistic religions there are good and evil spirits—gods and demons—struggling for control. According to biblical religion, however, evil is a corruption of the good. There is only one sovereign God—the triune God who created and sustains the world by the word of his power. He is good and is capable of creating only that which is good. "God is light; in him there is no darkness at all" (1 John 1:5), and he pronounced his creation "very good" in Genesis 1:31.

Yet God also gives to creatures intelligence and freedom to worship him or to rebel. Even Satan was once a glorious angelic servant. In a prophecy against the king of Tyre, we see one more example of how creatures turn God's good gifts into weapons:

> *You were blameless in your ways*
> *   from the day you were created*
> *   till wickedness was found in you.*
> *Through your widespread trade*
> *   you were filled with violence,*
> *   and you sinned.*
> *So I drove you in disgrace from the*
> *   mount of God,*
> *   and I expelled you, guardian cherub,*
> *   from among the fiery stones.*

Your heart became proud
on account of your beauty,
and you corrupted your wisdom
because of your splendor.
So I threw you to the earth;
I made a spectacle of you before kings. (Ezek 28:15–17)

Humans, created in God's image, wanted to be gods themselves, so they rebelled. Ever since this rebellion, the world has been a place where God's good gifts are turned into weapons against him and each other. Even natural evils—like hurricanes and earthquakes—are evidence of the whole creation's subjection to the curse of sin and death (Rom 8:20–22). If God were not good and great, moral and natural disasters would engulf us. We can only talk about evil because we really do experience the good. And this is only possible because God keeps evil in check. There are not two principles of good and evil, both with equal power; there is just one good creator. "And we know that in all things God works for the good of those who love him, who have been called according to his purpose" (Rom 8:28).

In pantheistic and polytheistic worldviews—not just ancient but also modern forms of paganism—evil is eternal. It's just the way things are and have always been. After all, nature is "red in tooth and claw." However, according to Scripture evil is not a timeless principle. It is the result of certain actions that can only be related by telling a story. Creation is good. Its corruption is the result of personal rebellion against God's good and great purposes. Yet he will overcome this evil because as a good God he wills to do so, and because as a great God he can accomplish it. He has already secured this victory objectively through Christ's death and resurrection.

In fact, everything that Jesus was doing in his earthly ministry was part of his triumph over Satan. He fended off Satan's temptation in the wilderness (Matt 4:1–11), cast out demons (Mark 1:21–28), and announced that he saw Satan fall like lightening from the heavenly courtroom (Luke 10:18). However powerful in his destructive capabilities, Satan is only a creature. He is not a deity. Nor is he an eternal principle. He is simply a glorious creature who corrupts God's gifts and then uses them as weapons against his Lord. And he will be finally and forever banished.

We are assured at the end of the story that evil will have no place in the new creation: "Then I heard what sounded like a great multitude, like the roar of rushing waters and like loud peals of thunder, shouting: 'Hallelujah! For our Lord God Almighty reigns'" (Rev 19:6).

So when I say that the Bible tackles the problem of evil by telling a story rather than by explaining an eternal principle, this is what I have in mind. Only at the end will we know the full scale of God's triumph over evil. And even then we will never know God's secrets beyond what he chooses to reveal to us.

TWO QUESTIONS

A T THIS POINT I hear you asking two questions.

1. *If God's intention has always been to defeat Satan and evil, why didn't he keep Satan and Adam from sinning in the first place?* A frequent answer is that God gave Satan and Adam the freedom to choose whether they would serve him. I have not found in Scripture any philosophical resolution to this problem. This suggests to me that it is beyond my ability to comprehend. Here I must simply affirm what Scripture does reveal: (1) God is not evil and cannot be tempted by evil; (2) nothing happens without God's knowledge and permission;

and (3) God never wills to permit any evil that he has not already determined to overcome.

2. Even if God allowed these acts, why didn't he end the reign of sin and death at the resurrection of Christ? God could have destroyed Satan, judged the world, and brought the cosmos into his everlasting reign of peace on Easter morning. However, this would have left us condemned. Having secured our redemption, Jesus ascended to the throne of all power and with the Father sent the Holy Spirit to open our hearts to receive Christ through faith.

United to him, we are justified and are being renewed daily. Every day of this stay of execution is a gracious reprieve, as millions of God's enemies are reconciled to him. In the meantime, the weeds in God's garden grow alongside the wheat. But Jesus tells us, as he told the disciples, not to pull up the weeds yet, "because while you are pulling the weeds, you may uproot the wheat with them. Let both grow together until the harvest. At that time I will tell the harvesters: First collect the weeds and tie them in bundles to be burned; then gather the wheat and bring it into my barn" (see Matt 13:24–30). God tolerates things as they are not because he is unjust, but because he is merciful and using this era to bring in his guests for the wedding feast of the Son and his bride.

For Christians, and only for Christians, evil is a *real* problem. I wrestle with it. If you believe in something or someone beyond "nature red in tooth and claw," then you do too. It's a nagging issue precisely because you do believe that there is more to reality than what you make of it. There's something "out there," beyond us and our choices and interpretations, that makes evil an intolerable conundrum. You cannot explain away evil because you can't explain away God. You cannot just get rid of the problem by getting rid of the idea of God.

If you do believe in God, the only answer—once again—is Jesus. In

Christ's life, death, resurrection, ascension, and second coming we see how God has dealt with sin and evil once and for all.

That there's no philosophical resolution to the problem of evil—from our vantage point here and now—shouldn't be surprising. Even Jesus's disciples didn't understand what God was doing at Calvary, with the saddest day in their lives being the day on which God actually triumphed over sin and death. No philosophical argument could lead them to believe that God was reconciling the world to himself in Christ on Good Friday. There's a *historical* resolution, though. Evil *is* overcome, not by us and our choices but by God and his decisions in Christ.

CHAPTER 4

GOD SPEAKS

DOES GOD TALK TO US? Lots of people think so. Some attract media attention for claiming to have died and returned from heaven with the details. Others say that God speaks to them every day in audible terms, telling them where to go and what to do. Maybe you wonder, "Why doesn't that happen to me?"

But the truth is it does happen to you—God still speaks to us today. But he does so through his Word. We speak to God in prayer and he speaks to us in the Bible. God especially speaks to us in the public gathering of his people each Lord's Day through the preaching of his Word.

THE WORD PREACHED

A LOT OF PEOPLE view preaching as a public scolding, or as someone merely venting his or her opinions about life, politics, and culture, or sharing personal experiences and helpful advice. Of course, there's no reason to go to church for that sort of thing. You may as well stay at home and watch TV, surf the Internet, or talk to a friend. But preaching is central to Christianity. The apostle Paul says, "Faith comes from hearing the message, and the message is heard through the word about Christ" (Rom 10:17). In fact, it's especially the gospel—"the word about Christ"—that is of earth-shaking and life-changing significance.

God speaks through the law to warn: you are "dead in your transgressions and sins" (Eph 2:1), "separate from Christ . . . without hope and without God" (Eph 2:12). It's through hearing God's word of law that we learn that to remain in this condition is to be under guilt, fear, and condemnation—not as a merely subjective feeling but as God's objective justice. Every one of us needs to hear this sober diagnosis. We're drunk with superficial well-wishing, spiritual hype, and a foolish optimism that refuses to face the fact that we die—"and after that to face judgment" (Heb 9:27). We don't want to hear it, perhaps, but it's founded on evidence.

Happily, God also announces good news. Sure, God's righteousness judges us as condemned rebels. "Therefore no one will be declared righteous in God's sight by the works of the law; rather, through the law we become conscious of our sin" (Rom 3:20). But that's not the end of the story: "But now apart from the law the righteousness of God has been made known, to which the Law and the Prophets testify. This righteousness is given through faith in Jesus Christ to all who believe" (Rom 3:21–22). In other words, the righteousness *of* God revealed in his law condemns us, but the righteousness *from* God is a gift that we have in Christ through faith. And faith comes to us through the preaching of the gospel.

We get the law at least to some extent. We have some sense of right and wrong. We even think that people who do bad things shouldn't be let off the hook. When it comes to dealing with guilt, people have elaborate rituals for trying to pacify the gods. Some have even sacrificed their children. In more sophisticated societies we have psychologists or even preachers who try to convince us that guilt is an illusion. People either deny God completely or try to placate him by promising to do better in the future to make up for mistakes. But the bad news is like hearing, "You have cancer." It's a fact, not just a feeling.

Yet out of his love the Father sent his own Son to become one of us, to live a righteous life, and to bear our judgment *in our place*. The Son did this freely, laying down his life for us (John 10:15). We need to hear this good news constantly and that's why we need regular preaching, "fixing our eyes on Jesus, the pioneer and perfecter of faith. For the joy set before him he endured the cross, scorning its shame, and sat down at the right hand of the throne of God" (Heb 12:2).

The gospel is not wishful thinking. It's not just optimistic or sentimental uplift. It's the announcement of a fact. As good news, this message has to be announced or proclaimed. The Word of God is speech. That's what preaching is: telling us the truth about who God is, what he requires of us, where we stand with him, what he has done to save us in his Son, and how we are to live in the light of his marvelous gift.

So, yes, God does speak to us. But he speaks publicly, through preaching, because the bad news and the good news are not just private feelings but facts of universal significance. This is not to dismiss the wonderful truth that he also speaks to us as we read Scripture and talk to other believers about its teaching. Yet the main thing is to hear God address us regularly through the ministry of fellow believers who are called by God to study and proclaim his Word. God has chosen to use "the weak things of the world" as a means of his powerful working (1 Cor 1:27–28) so that he can receive all the glory (vv. 29–30).

God speaks to us through his Word in a variety of ways. He threatens, promises, comforts, discomforts, judges, justifies, kills, and makes alive by his Word, which is "alive and active" (Heb 4:12). The Holy Spirit is at work in us to open our eyes and hearts to his saving message. In speaking his law, God does two things. First, he arraigns us before his bar of judgment, showing us our sins so that we will flee to Christ to be clothed in his righteousness. But second, he also guides us by his law in the path of righteousness, loving him and our neighbors in concrete ways. No longer "under the law" in the sense of condemnation, we are free for the first time for love and good works—not to gain God's favor or to score points by helping others, but simply and truly for God's glory and our neighbor's good.

From Genesis to Revelation, God speaks to us. He especially proclaims his Son as the offspring of the woman (Eve) who crushes the serpent's head (Gen 3:15); as Noah's ark; as the ram caught in the thicket who took Isaac's place on the altar of sacrifice; as the greater prophet that Moses expected; as the promised Son of David whose throne is eternal; as the King greater than the weak and false kings throughout Israel's history; as the true temple; as "the Lamb of God, who takes away the sin of the world" (John 1:29).

What is the main reason I embrace the Bible as God's Word? It is hard to reduce my confidence in Scripture to one reason. Most fundamentally, I hear God address me in the Bible, especially in the preaching of his Word. Written by diverse authors over two millennia, the Bible nevertheless has a unity that can be attributed only to a divine author. It truly reads as promise (Old Testament) and fulfillment (New Testament), like any good story. Yet it is the greatest story ever told.

Meticulously detailed prophecies, fulfilled centuries later in Jesus Christ, cannot possibly refer to anyone but him. Through Scripture I have been brought to see the world and myself as created by God for his glory, to see that I am sinful and cannot save myself, and to know the Father no longer as his enemy but as a forgiven and adopted son in Jesus Christ.

Through this Word, I am regularly introduced to a wisdom that is beyond anything that I have ever encountered anywhere else. His commands are just, and his gospel is liberating. Through this Word, the futile character in the script that I have written for my life movie has died and has been raised to new life in the story of Jesus. Then there are all the others he has cast in his unfolding drama who have become my nearest of kin, more dear to me than blood relatives. We have been baptized into Christ together by one Spirit, share one faith, and partake of the same heavenly food and drink. As in any relationship, communication is key. The more I hear God speak to me in his Word, the more I come to know him. I trust God's Word for all these reasons and more.

However, it is one thing to offer reasons for my embracing Scripture and growing in my confidence in God's Word; it is quite another to put forth reasons for the Bible as God's Word. Even if I had never embraced it as such, the Bible is God's Word because it is authoritative, inerrant, clear, and sufficient.

WHERE DID THE BIBLE COME FROM?

RECALL THE STORY SO FAR, especially the evidence for Christ's resurrection that we examined in the first chapter. If Jesus is who he said he was and accomplished everything that the prophets foretold, then his views about the Bible must be ours.

Jesus assumed as historical truth the creation of the human race "at the beginning" as male and female, "one flesh" in the covenant of marriage (Matt 19:4–5). He treated Abel and Zechariah as historical figures who encompassed the whole of Old Testament history (Matt 23:35). The stories of Noah and the flood and the destruction of Sodom he regarded as historical events (Luke 17:26–30), as well as the stories of God's miraculous provision of manna in the wilderness (John 6:49) and of Jonah being swallowed by the large fish (Matt 12:39–40).

Jesus said that to hear the apostles is to hear Jesus himself and to receive them is to receive the Father and the Son (Matt 16:16–19; 18:18; 28:16–20; Acts 1:8). The apostles themselves understood that they were speaking authoritatively in Christ's name. Despite some friction early on, Peter acknowledges Paul's writings as "Scripture" (2 Pet 3:15–16), and Paul calls Luke's writings "Scripture" in 1 Timothy 5:18 (cf. Luke 10:7).

🔎 THE CANON

The canon is a collection of varied texts that are authoritative for the followers of a religion. When we call the Bible a canon, we mean that its books are united by their divine Source (the Father's speaking), their content (the Son's work of redemption), and their power to generate the world of which they speak (the Spirit's work of inspiration, illumination, and regeneration).

So to summarize the argument: (1) Jesus is God incarnate; (2) Jesus appealed to Old Testament Scripture as authoritative, inerrant, clear, and as being fulfilled in his ministry; and (3) Jesus authorized his apostles to speak in his name, and they recognized their written records and epistles—and those of each other—as God's Word. Taken together, these writings are called a "canon" (from the Greek *kanōn*, "rule"), the norm for faith and practice.

The Bible did not fall from heaven. Typically, God works through means and over time. Remember when Jesus healed the blind man by mixing his spit with the dirt and placing the mud in the man's eyes (John 9:1–7)? He could simply have waved his hand but instead used the matter that he had created. That is the way God has always worked his miracles. He saved Noah and his family through a huge boat, giving explicit instructions on how to build it and with what materials. He made Moses his ambassador to Pharaoh and gave Moses a rod to split the Red Sea. Wherever his ark of the covenant went, there was victory in battle. His Spirit took up residence in the temple. God used ordinary people, places, and things to fulfill his extraordinary plans.

The same is true of the Bible. It's a fully human collection of sixty-six books, written by very different authors across very different times and places. The Bible itself reveals its human authorship on every page. The prophets foretold far more than they themselves understood (1 Pet 1:10–12). They are revealed as weak and sinful human beings, just like us. They lacked understanding and information about a host of matters. In no instance does God put the prophets and apostles in a trance. Nor, at least in most cases, were they merely taking dictation. It was their words, their thoughts, their way of expressing things that they put into writing. And yet its source ultimately was God. They were given no crystal balls or tea leaves to read in order to divine the future. They were never in control of the prophecy. Instead, they were uprooted from their ordinary callings by the voice of God and spoke only when God gave them something to say. What they said was not for their personal edification but for public announcement. They were God's ambassadors.

The technical term for this traditional Christian understanding of Scripture is *inspiration*—specifically, *verbal-plenary inspiration*—which means that the very words of Scripture and not just its main ideas are God's. It is "God-breathed" (2 Tim 3:16). As such, it is *inerrant*. The Spirit so guided the biblical writers that, as Peter declares, "prophecy never had its origin in the human will, but prophets, though human, spoke from God as they were carried along by the Holy Spirit" (2 Pet 1:21). As God's ambassadors, they did not speak their own hunches and advice. Rather, they simply heard the voice of God and conveyed what he told them.

But there is a lot more in the Bible than prophecy. In many cases we read nothing of God's direct communication. There are histories, songs, dialogues, parables, and other forms of writing. Luke tells us that he compiled his Gospel after interviewing a host of living eyewitnesses to Jesus's ministry. And just as Jesus entered fully into our humanity, so he reveals himself through the apostles by their testimony to what they saw and heard (1 John 1:1–4).

🔍 **VERBAL-PLENARY INSPIRATION**

God is the ultimate author of Scripture and Scripture is inspired—that is, "God-breathed" (2 Tim 3:16)—in its words and in its entirety. An *organic* view of inspiration recognizes the fully human character of Scripture, evident in the diversity of style, interest, and cultural-linguistic context of each author. It is from God yet written through human beings, compiled over many centuries.

THE ROLE OF SCRIPTURE

UNLIKE THE CHURCH, Scripture is inerrant (without error in all that it affirms) and self-consistent.[9] When people say that the Bible contradicts itself, you have to ask for specifics. Where are those contradictions? For example, if the Old Testament forbids the eating of pork and the New Testament allows it, is that a contradiction? Not at all. The Old Testament prophets tell us of a day when God will make "a new covenant" that will include Jews and Gentiles. The church will no longer be a geo-political nation, but an international community of those who through faith are children of Abraham. Thus, the laws connected with the old covenant theocracy are now "obsolete" (Heb 8:13). That is not a contradiction, but a change in administration from the Old to the New Testament.

There are tougher difficulties to be sure. There are apparent discrepancies between the Gospels in reports of the events surrounding Christ's resurrection. Yet that is precisely what one would expect from eyewitnesses. Each viewed the same event from different vantage points and even at different moments of its unfolding. A competent judge's suspicions would be aroused if all the defense's witnesses in a trial said exactly the same thing. It would suggest that they were not testifying to what actually happened but crafting an account that smoothed over any differences. However, none of the discrepancies in the Gospels has any bearing on the claim made by all the evangelists that Jesus rose from the dead.

WHAT DO WE EXPECT TO FIND IN THE BIBLE?

E VEN AMONG THOSE who share the same view of biblical authority and inerrancy, there are often different interpretations of texts, and such differences will not be eliminated until Christ returns. Nevertheless, it helps to know what you're looking for in the Bible.

Some treat the Bible as a divine sourcebook for science. To be sure, whatever it explicitly affirms on such matters is to be received. But did God intend through his prophets and apostles to deliver scientific theories? When we go to the Bible with our questions, demanding that it speak to whatever we find important or relevant, we force it to say things that it does not actually address. For example, as John Calvin observed, Moses was not an astronomer and the Pentateuch is not a science textbook. Whatever Scripture does teach explicitly about such matters is authoritative, but its *purpose* is not to provide a secret code for determining the age of the earth, the orbit of planets, or precise details concerning the earth's condition prior to the creation of human beings.

Some come to Scripture trying to correlate the Bible's prophecies with the daily headlines. However, the Old Testament prophets were pointing to Christ (1 Pet 1:10–12). Jesus's own prophetic teaching turned on his crucifixion, resurrection, ascension, and return in glory (e.g., Matt 24–25). Revelation comforts persecuted saints in all times and places with the triumph of the Lamb in a consummated kingdom without sin and death.

INERRANCY

As "God-breathed," Scripture has historically been held by Christians to be free of error. Inerrancy pertains to the original texts, not our translations or copies. However, the immense number of ancient copies allows textual scholars to determine the original readings with near certainty. Inerrancy does not cancel out human agency nor does it imply that the human authors were omniscient or perfect in their understanding. Scripture is inerrant in all that it affirms, but this does not mean the human authors were exhaustive or exact, a caution against imposing modern standards of exactitude upon ancient texts.

Others call the Bible "the owner's manual" or "the roadmap for life." Or they turn to Scripture expecting to find a catalogue of moral advice for practical living, turning parables of the kingdom into quarries for defending capitalism or socialism, managing personal finances and family life, and so forth. There is no doubt that Scripture provides direction, but is it mainly a book of ethics? If we go to the Bible looking for answers to questions that are beyond its purpose and scope, we will turn it into an entirely different book, as did the Pharisees to whom Jesus said: "You study the Scriptures diligently because you think that in them you have eternal life. These are the very Scriptures that testify about me, yet you refuse to come to me to have life" (John 5:39–40).

When we rifle through the Old Testament narratives for moral examples ("Dare to be a Daniel"), as if they were like Aesop's fables, we miss the point. In most cases the lives of "Bible heroes" are quite mixed, morally speaking. And in every narrative, God is the real hero of the story. David slays Goliath not because he possesses superhuman strength but because the Spirit comes upon him. In each instance, the purpose of the narrative is not to provide life lessons that we may apply directly to ourselves, but to see how God is fulfilling his purposes that lead history to Jesus Christ. It is certainly true that the Bible includes wisdom for daily living (especially in Ecclesiastes, Proverbs, and Song of Solomon), but even these books direct us ultimately to Jesus Christ, "who has become for us wisdom from God—that is, our righteousness, holiness and redemption" (1 Cor 1:30).

The scope of Scripture therefore is God's commands and promises—law and gospel—centering on this unfolding plan in Jesus Christ. It is crucial to recognize this point because we easily turn the Bible into a "handbook for life," an answer book or manual of supernatural information on anything that interests us.

Instead we must allow Scripture itself to identify *its* scope and purpose. We have to come to Scripture with humility, allowing it to give us its own questions as well as answers. This means that we need to interpret Scripture in its natural sense, recognizing the differences in genre between historical narrative and apocalyptic, poetry and prose, parable, and doctrinal exposition. We also need to recognize the difference between covenants based on law and covenants based on promise, and covenants that are no longer in effect and covenants that are everlasting. In short, we come to Scripture expecting it to testify centrally to the interests that it has already displayed. Each passage has to be interpreted in the light of the whole while doing justice to each part.

A FOUNDING AND RULING CONSTITUTION

IN MY NATION'S HISTORY a revolutionary war was fought over independence from Great Britain. However, to be liberated *from* one power is not yet to be a nation. Only with the writing and signing of the US Constitution was the republic established. As its name suggests, such a founding document literally "constitutes" an independent people as interdependent states with a national capital.

In a similar way, Christ's victory liberated us from the powers of death and hell. Yet Christ has also formed us into his new covenant people through a New Testament. This canon became the constitution that determines the faith and practice of this peculiar organism called "the church."

To continue the analogy, the apostles were our "founding fathers." Through them our Lord established his constitution, his canon. This is why Paul refers to their labors as the foundation-laying episode in our history. There is no more foundation-laying after the apostles. They have no successors. Rather, ordinary ministers now build on that foundation and their ministry is judged by how faithfully they build upon it. None of us is a Moses. None is a Paul or a Peter. The apostolic era was a unique stage of history and the apostles held a unique office, called by God for the drafting of the new covenant constitution.

Today the Spirit illumines the hearts and minds of God's people to understand, interpret, and obey his Word. As we see in the report of the Council of Jerusalem (Acts 15), pastors and elders today continue to gather from each church to interpret God's Word on particular matters. These assemblies function like courts of law. To continue our analogy, they operate like the federal judiciary, interpreting the Constitution with no power to add to or subtract from it.

Faith comes through the Word publicly proclaimed (Rom 10:17). It is the Word that gives birth to the church, not vice versa. As the Word is read publicly in church and in family and private worship, we are shaped by it. As a written text, Scripture is the final judge for doctrine, worship, and life. Apart from this gracious work of the Spirit through this one Word, each believer and the church corporately would eventually become a tower of Babel rather than an organized society of the new creation as we see at Pentecost.

Despite the tragic divisions in Christ's visible body today, there remains a remarkable consensus on the basic teachings of Scripture across many churches and denominations. Precisely because Scripture is "God-breathed" and is therefore not only infallible but clear in its basic teachings, we are confident that the Spirit-illumined church will be able to interpret it faithfully from generation to generation.

CHAPTER 5

GOD MADE THE WORLD BUT WE'VE MADE A MESS OF IT

A FRIEND FROM COLLEGE lost her daughter to leukemia. Through tears she told me, "I don't know if I can believe in a God who made such a messed-up world as this." As a pastor I've learned that in those times when I hear people say things like this, it's often better for me just to listen. We do not always believe everything we say in our laments; they express how we feel in the moment. Nevertheless, her sentiment is one that many people do believe even apart from those moments of pain and anger. There are plenty of people who think that if there is a Creator, he is not very good at his job.

But there is a Creator, and he created everything that exists *by his speech*:

> *By the word of the Lord the heavens were made,*
> *their starry host by the breath of his mouth. . . .*
> *For he spoke, and it came to be;*
> *he commanded, and it stood firm. (Ps 33:6, 9)*
> *The Mighty One, God, the Lord,*
> *speaks and summons the earth*
> *from the rising of the sun to where it sets. (Ps 50:1)*

God spoke all the material of creation into existence from nothing. Additionally, his speech shapes creaturely response. In other words, God doesn't just act *upon* creation; he acts *within* it, as we see in the rich imagery of the Spirit sweeping across the earth with his fructifying energies. This same Spirit now gives us new life and indwells and renews us, and this shapes the kind of sovereignty and reign that God exercises. Our God is not a distant monarch who merely barks orders. Because he is the Father, the Son, and the Spirit, our God is above us, among us, and within us, bringing his word to pass.

ROYAL DIGNITY: WHAT IT MEANS TO BE HUMAN

MODERN ASTRONOMY introduces us to an inconceivably vast cosmos. Earth's galaxy the Milky Way contains an estimated 100 to 400 billion stars and 100 billion planets. Until the 1920s astronomers thought that ours was the only galaxy. Yet after Edwin Hubble's research, we now know that the Milky Way is but one of billions of galaxies.

Stargazing with the naked eye was enough to provoke the psalmist's wonder:

When I consider your heavens, the work of your fingers,
the moon and the stars, which you have set in place,
what is mankind that you are mindful of them,
human beings that you care for them? (Ps 8:3–4)

This question—"What is mankind that you are mindful of them?"—is placed within a covenantal context. It is not abstract speculation. The psalmist questions the reason for human existence, but he cannot do so apart from reference to God. Why does God care about this slight creature? The answer comes in the form of a creation story where God creates human beings "a little lower than the angels" (v. 5), yet with royal dignity.

The royal dignity of the first human beings encompassed both body and soul. As we have seen, there are only two fundamental categories: God and everything else—the creator and his creation. Our souls are not some form of the divine spark within us. We are not by nature immortal. Rather, God gives immortality as a gift to the whole person—soul and body. Although the soul survives bodily death (Luke 23:43; 2 Cor 5:1–10; Phil 1:21–24; Rev 6:9–10), it is only with the reintegration of body and soul in the resurrection that the whole person is finally saved (Rom 8:23; 1 Cor 15:1–55).

There are two important words we must learn at this point: *covenant* and *eschatology*.

Covenant refers to the *context* in which God created us. If God is King, Adam was his

 COVENANT AND ESCHATOLOGY

A covenant is an oath-based union given under stipulations and sanctions. The covenant of creation (or works) was between God and humanity in Adam. Disobedience to this covenant by Adam led to death for all humanity. The covenant of grace is between the triune God and Christ and his church, with Christ as the mediator. In this covenant God promises to be our God and to make believers and their children his own redeemed family.

Eschatology refers to the goal of creation and the unfolding of God's purposes as we move toward the climax of history.

prime minister. Appointing Adam as the covenantal head of the human race, God issued his decree to him that he should faithfully execute every word that comes from the mouth of the great King.

The other word we need to know is eschatology. This refers to the *goal of God creating human beings*. Creation was just the beginning of a relationship that would lead either to covenantal blessing or curse, everlasting life or death. The tree of life lay up ahead as the reward for covenantal obedience. By fulfilling the commission that God gave him, Adam would have won for himself and his posterity not merely a continuance of temporal blessing but entrance into God's everlasting Sabbath rest. Swept up in Adam's train, the whole creation would enjoy forever the liberty of God's children.

The image of God (*imago Dei*) is not something *in* us, a semi-divine substance, but something *between* us and God that constitutes a covenantal relationship. To put it a little differently, the image of God is not something that we *have* somewhere inside of us; it is what we *are*. We are very image conscious these days. Yet unless you know what the original looks like (namely, God), you will waste your time gazing at your own reflection in the mirror. Like Narcissus in the Greek myth, falling in love with your own reflection in the pond becomes a fateful prison.

Human beings are God's viceroys, his representatives among the creatures he made. Especially in creating human beings as his image—both male and female—God produces an analogy of himself as the communion of three persons in love. To be a human being is therefore to be God's image. It is to hold a high covenantal office, maintaining God's good order of love, righteousness, holiness, and justice. Everyone is aware of this divine calling. Even false religions could not exist except as a distortion of general revelation and the covenant of creation. This moral law is etched on the conscience. Consequently, all people "are without excuse" (Rom 1:20). Indeed, "the whole world" is "held guilty" on the basis of this original covenant with its law still inscribed on the conscience. Adam was created in righteousness and true holiness, but he was not yet confirmed in everlasting justice and blessing. It was his vocation as the representative head of humanity to fulfill his covenantal trial and win the right to eat from the tree of life.

THE SERVANT'S TREASON

ADAM'S REPRESENTATIVE HEADSHIP is the source of both the grandeur and the tragedy of our existence. Genesis 3 provides the evidence for the case of "Yahweh v. Humanity." Even before the infamous act of eating the forbidden fruit, Adam and Eve failed to execute their office.

First, Adam and Eve refused to exercise their royal dominion. Instead of driving God's enemy from God's garden, they allowed the serpent to enter into the covenantal conversation. In one sense Satan is a great lawyer in God's courtroom. Once the most beautiful angel in God's court, Satan aspired to the throne itself. He is the one who "accuses [the saints] before our God day and night" (Rev 12:10). He is "a liar and the father of lies" (John 8:44). Once the chief magistrate under God in heaven, he has become the archetype and ruler of false witnesses on earth. He is superb in his logic and rhetoric. He even knows how to quote Scripture. Yet in all of this princely eloquence he perverts, twists, and corrupts God's Word. God alone is the creator. Satan is not original. He can only work with the good words and deeds of God as the raw material that he then corrupts. He cannot say or do anything new. His lies are parasitical on the truth. So he begins with just enough of God's word, in order to twist it (as he did—this time unsuccessfully—in Jesus's temptation). It was Satan who first corrupted God's word by addition, then by subtraction, and then finally by direct contradiction.

Adam is not absent from the scene when the serpent approaches and addresses Eve. In fact, he "was with her" (Gen 3:6). But he passively and silently observed the conversation, exposing his irresponsible sloth. Eve begins well, correcting Satan's obvious misquotation of God's command about eating from the tree, but then she adds her own clause: "God did say, 'You must not eat fruit from the tree that is in the middle of the garden, *and you must not touch it*, or you will die'" (Gen 3:3; emphasis added). Satan then directly contradicts God's word: "You will not certainly die. . . . For God knows that when you eat from it your eyes will be opened, and you will be like God, knowing good and evil" (vv. 4–5).

This appeal to autonomous pride has been successful ever since. Notice the emphasis on Eve's action as guided by what she saw, felt, and approved: "When the woman saw that the fruit of the tree was good for food and pleasing to the eye, and also desirable for gaining wisdom, she took some and ate it. She also gave some to her husband, who was with her, and he ate it" (v. 6).

Think of all the ways in which our culture of advertising promises products that will enlighten us. Tickling our ears, they tell us that we're worth it, that we deserve it, and that we shouldn't let anything or anyone stand in the way of our self-fulfillment and self-realization. But Adam and Eve were not enlightened by listening to the serpent's lies; instead they were darkened in their understanding. Their eyes were opened, but to the horrible truth. Once naked and unashamed, they were now appalled by their sinfulness, which the fading glory of their bodies now revealed. Their solution was as superficial as their diagnosis, as they strung together fig leaves for coverings (v. 7).

Although the serpent seduced the royal couple with the false promise of autonomy, he knew that autonomy was impossible. His real intent was to make them his image bearers rather than God's. Satan still uses this tactic with us. First he adds to God's word to make the command sound more burdensome. Then he subtracts by encouraging us to question whether God really said what we think he did. Finally, he goes in for the kill: God is wrong. In fact, God is deceiving you in order to keep you under his thumb.

Instead of hearing God's word, Adam and Eve sought to see, control, master, and determine it for themselves (Gen 3:3–6). Like Satan himself, they began to employ the official endowments of their holy office for treason. The excellencies of the image were not eradicated, but each was deformed. Our powerful dominion has now become violent tyranny. Pure love has become warped by greedy self-interest and our enormous capacities for sociality—no longer shaped by hearing God's word—have become laced with half-truths, resentment, and misleading communication. The garden of Eden became a tower of Babel. Each aspect of the image-office was corrupted by the fall.

God caught up with Adam and Eve after their treason, demanding an account of what they had done. Why were they running from God? "I heard you in the garden, and I was afraid because I was naked; so I hid" (v. 10). This has been the tragic response of the human conscience in the presence of God ever since.

The fact that we are still office holders in the covenant of creation and that the image, while corrupted, was not lost at the fall is in one sense a blessing. It serves as the foundation for upholding the dignity of every person. In another sense, however, it is a curse because it means that everyone is born into the world under obligation yet marred by a refusal to honor that obligation.

As soon as we are born, we are already moving toward death. We cannot resign our office or refuse to relate with God. We cannot remain in hiding or escape the approaching footsteps of the covenant Lord. As prophets we are false witnesses, as priests we serve idols, and as kings we yield our allegiance to evil counselors. When vested with power, we abuse it for our own good rather than use it for the good of others. We are all glorious ambassadors guilty of high treason.

THE KING'S SENTENCE

IN EVERY SUBPLOT OF THE BIBLE we discover echoes of the trial of the covenant servant in the cosmic courtroom. When gathered at the foot of Sinai and filled with terror by the divine words, the Israelites entreated Moses, "Speak to us yourself and we will listen. But do not have God speak to us or we will die" (Exod 20:19). Like Adam, Israel was also on trial. The holy land was a gift but Israel was on probation. Even the prophet Isaiah, caught up in a vision of God in holy splendor, could only reply, "Woe to me . . . I am ruined!" (Isa 6:5). It was this same terror that gripped Peter's conscience after he witnessed Jesus calming the storm. He could only say, "Go away from me, Lord; I am a sinful man!" (Luke 5:8).

Adam in his disobedience took the witness stand against God. Denying the witness of the Spirit, the testimony of the whole creation, and even the glory, beauty, and integrity of his own high office, Adam perjured himself. Again, this helps us to better define and understand the nature of evil. Evil is not a principle in creation itself but is the willful distortion of good gifts into an arsenal deployed against God's reign. This perversity corrupts that which is noble, suppresses that which is righteous, smears that which is beautiful, and smothers the light of truth. Every sign of human oppression, violence, idolatry, and immorality in the world can be seen as the perversion of an original good. Our original commission to be fruitful and multiply and to guard, protect, and subdue God's garden so that its peace and righteousness extend to the ends of the earth is now twisted into empires of oppression that exercise violence in order to secure a heaven without God.

Pain in childbirth is dreaded in any circumstance, yet this part of God's judgment was particularly directed to Eve: "I will make your pains in childbearing very severe; with painful labor you will give birth to children" (Gen 3:16). The increased pain she experienced undoubtedly included the emotional stress of bringing children into a world that was now fallen and would be increasingly filled with violence, deprivation, and depravity. God indicates that she will also experience disruption in her relationship with Adam: "Your desire will be for your husband, and he will rule over you" (v. 16). Enmity with God draws into its wake enmity against fellow humans, including husband and wife.

The entire covenantal fabric of human life has now become brittle and broken. To be sure, childbirth and marriage remain joyful experiences because God has not entirely abandoned humanity to its own devices. The order and purpose of God's creation remain, upheld by God's hand. And yet these common gifts are a mixed blessing. They involve pain and futility. The curse imposed upon Adam and the ground is commensurate with the fruitlessness and vanity that life now yields to human experience. Created to have dominion over the earth in order to bring forth its fruitfulness, creation itself now turns its back on those who have turned their back on their covenant Lord.

Adam blamed Eve, Eve blamed the serpent, and at the end of the day we all blame God, following this course of vanity. In ancient and modern dualism, the problem of evil is identified with created nature in an effort to externalize sin by attributing it to the "other," whether "the woman you put here with me," our physical or social environment, our family, or other circumstances beyond our control. But ultimately, we are blaming God. We look for scapegoats to avoid our guilt. The murder of six million Jews in the Holocaust displays how far humans can go in trying to find others to blame for the world's ills.

Instead of using our keen minds and noble passions to find our rest in God, we deploy them as weapons against him. The accused are discovered fleeing the scene of the crime, covering up the evidence. All are now born into the world "dead in . . . transgressions and sins" and "by nature deserving of wrath" (Eph 2:1, 3). Instead of representing the interests of the great King in the world, his ambassadors have defected to the enemy. Driven deeper into the brush, we suppress the truth about ourselves and our relationship with God.

The law was once given to Adam as the way to everlasting life, yet now there is only the expectation of death and judgment. The law announces this word of condemnation to everyone who is under it, whether in its written form or as it has been inscribed on the conscience, "so that every mouth may be silenced and the whole world held accountable to God" (Rom 3:19).

The accusation pronounced by God's law—however it is rebuffed, rationalized, therapeutically suppressed, or ignored through distraction—rings in the conscience and, as psychologist Robert Jay Lifton observes, drives our sense of guilt for a fault whose source seems forever ambiguous.[10] Thinking that their problem was merely shame rather than guilt, Adam and Eve covered themselves with loincloths, and ever since their feeble attempts we have found ourselves incapable—or rather, unwilling—to accept the radical diagnosis of our own depravity. We talk about evil outside of us, the "others," whoever they may be. We blame evil places, structures, forces, and principles. But, like the religious leaders whom Jesus challenged, we refuse to locate evil within ourselves (Matt 12:33–37; 15:10–20; 23:25–28).

The accused, after offering countersuits and blaming each other for their faults, now face their sentence (Gen 3:14–19). In all these sanctions the generous giving and receiving embedded in God's natural order will yield to strife, control, exploitation, and manipulation at every level.

Instead of being confirmed in righteousness and everlasting life, Adam and his posterity will return to the dust (v. 19).

Humanity in Adam is now a false prophet who misrepresents God's Word in a futile and treasonous demand for autonomy. We have become false priests who corrupt God's sanctuary instead of guarding, keeping, and extending it. And we are now false kings who are no longer the agents of God's loving reign but who have unleashed a cruel tyranny over the earth and each other.

WHAT DOES THIS HAVE TO DO WITH YOU?

EVERY PERSON is now born estranged from the good Father, living in the far country in poverty and degradation. Unwilling to be God's faithful son, humanity has become a slave of sin and death.

Reading Genesis 3 in the light of the whole biblical story brings into sharper focus the corporate and representational character of Adam's covenantal role. Not only was Adam in covenant with God, but all humanity is in covenant with God with Adam as our covenant head. Indeed, all of creation was in some sense also judged in Adam (Gen 3:17–18; Rom 8:20).

This means that we stand or fall together. The legal and relational basis for this solidarity is the covenant of creation. Our collective human estrangement is often referred to as *original sin*. This doctrine teaches that we are all heirs of Adam's *guilt* and *corruption*.

Paul elaborates on this covenantal outlook when he explains that "sin entered the world through one man," in whom all people became henceforth sinners, condemned by the law and inwardly corrupt (Rom 5:12–21). Since Adam failed to carry out his commission as the servant-king of Yahweh, all those who are "in Adam" are implicated as well.

PELAGIUS

ORIGINAL SIN

At the turn of the fifth century, a British monk named Pelagius wanted to improve Christian morals and taught that humans are born in the same condition as Adam, with the free will to determine whether they will obey or disobey God's commands. If they obey they will be saved. Adam is just a bad example to avoid, and Jesus is our redeemer who provides instruction and an example of godly living. It was the original self-help gospel. By contrast, the church has taught that sin is the fallen condition of all humanity with legal and transformative aspects. We are both guilty and corrupt as a result of Adam's sin.

As the biblical drama unfolds, we see with increasing clarity that original sin makes us all equally condemned and corrupt.

If you only make "mistakes," you simply need better instruction, examples, and encouragement. Even if you commit "crimes," you may require incarceration or therapy to improve. But mistakes and crimes are not our primary problems. The wrongs that we do are called *sins* because they are first and foremost rebellions against God.

After committing adultery with Bathsheba and then sending her husband into battle to face certain death, David confessed to the Lord, "Against you, you only, have I sinned and done what is evil in your sight; so you are right in your verdict and justified when you judge" (Ps 51:4). As heinous as his crimes against others were, their true depravity must be measured by the fact that they were sins against God. David realized, as his confession shows, that he had not merely made a mistake. And he had not simply done sinful things. The true problem is his inherent corruption: "Surely I was sinful at birth, sinful from the time my mother conceived me" (v. 5). We are not sinners because we sin; we sin because we are sinners. To solve a problem this pervasive and endemic, we need nothing less than divine rescue. The dead need more than just a little makeup; they must be raised to life.

Religion is one of the "fig leaves" we use to cover up our shame instead of actually dealing with the guilt that gives rise to it. Many people attend churches where, week after week, they hear positive messages and have their egos boosted. They are told that we are not helpless sinners who need a radical salvation; we are good people who need a little help to do a little better. We project a god who will satisfy our suppression of the truth about ourselves (Rom 1:18). In our proud moral striving, our self-confident religious devotion, and our sincere pretensions, we are storing up God's wrath against us.

Upbeat popular culture, feeding on images of the beautiful, well-adjusted, pleasant, happy, young, and vigorous, ignores the brutal reality of life. Yet it is the reality of our pain and suffering that is the trigger-mechanism for the biblical hope of the gospel. In the doctrine of original sin, biblical faith comes to grips with the reality of human tragedy and transforms the tragic drama into the joyful comedy of which pagan revelry is only a pale parody. Jesus asked:

> *To what, then, can I compare the people of this generation? What are they like? They are like children sitting in the marketplace and calling out to each other:*
>
> *"We played the pipe for you, and you did not dance;*
> *we sang a dirge, and you did not cry."*
>
> *For John the Baptist came neither eating bread nor drinking wine, and you say, "He has a demon." The Son of Man came eating and drinking, and you say, "Here is a glutton and a drunkard, a friend of tax collectors and sinners." (Luke 7:31–34)*

The law slays us. It yields that inescapable "guilty" verdict. But the Pharisees, "confident of their own righteousness," were not ready for a funeral (Luke 18:9). They could not mourn, yet they were unable to dance. Consequently they could not join gladly in the wedding reception! Only those who have been brought to the end of their spiritual rope will finally let themselves fall into the everlasting arms of a merciful Savior and see their mourning turned to dancing.

HOW *TOTAL* IS TOTAL DEPRAVITY?

THIS STARK BIBLICAL VIEW of original sin is sometimes called "total depravity." "Depravity" comes from the Latin *pravus*, meaning "crooked, perverse." It is the twisting of something straight, the corruption of something good. As we have seen, sin is always a distortion of something good. When we say that this distortion and corruption is "total," we are not saying that we are as bad as we possibly can be. We mean that it affects the whole person. It means that there is no aspect of our existence that is left unspoiled by the sinful condition. Our mind, heart, will, body, and desires are all in agreement against God. Total depravity means that there is no part of us that lies outside the bondage of sin and death.

This does not mean that the essence of our humanity is evil or that its created nature has been lost. We cannot blame God or some aspect of our being, such as our body and its passions. God created these drives and they are good. And far from being impossible, everything that God demands of us is within our natural ability as originally designed and created. The fault lies with our inherent moral corruption, which now perverts these good impulses, thoughts, and desires.

This means that even the best works of believers are stained with sin.

"All of us have become like one who is unclean, and all our righteous acts are like filthy rags; we all shrivel up like a leaf, and like the wind our sins sweep us away" (Isa 64:6). Moreover, Paul says, "everything that does not come from faith is sin" (Rom 14:23).

But surely things cannot be this bad. Deep down we are good people, we tell ourselves. We may have done some things we're not proud of, but we have "good hearts," good intentions. No, God replies, "The heart is deceitful *above all things* and beyond cure" (Jer 17:9; emphasis added). Jesus excoriated the religious leaders for imagining that there was some innocent citadel of righteousness in the mind or heart, countering instead that it is from this seat that sin exercises its dominion (Matt 12:34–35; 15:10–11; 23:25). The inner self is not an innocent spark of divinity or an island of purity. It is the fountain from which every act of violence, deceit, immorality, and idolatry flows out through the body and into the world.

It is helpful to clarify a few distinctions here. Everyone has the *natural* ability to render to God faithful obedience. In other words, we cannot blame God for creating human beings with a faulty part or a weakness of nature. We were designed and created with integrity—no errors or faults. After the fall, however, we lost the *moral* ability to attain the righteousness that God requires.

 TOTAL DEPRAVITY AND OUR ABILITY

Total depravity does not mean that we are incapable of anything good before our fellow humans. It says that there is nothing within us that is left unfallen from which we might begin to bargain or to restore our condition. It does not mean that every person will indulge in every form of sin or that we cannot admire virtuous character. Humans still possess a conscience and can discriminate between good and evil. We are free to will and choose what our mind and heart desire, but our mind has been darkened and our heart is selfish. Everyone has a natural ability to render God faithful obedience, but after the fall our moral ability is held captive to our own selfishness and idolatry. The fault lies not in that we cannot but that we will not turn from our sin to the living God.

We are "sold as a slave to sin," held captive not by a foreign army but by our own selfishness, idolatry, greed, and deceit (Rom 7:14). "There is no one righteous, not even one; there is no one who understands; there is no one who seeks God" (Rom 3:10–11). This is not mere hyperbole. Even when we pretend to seek God, we are running from the God who is actually there. If the self-help sections of the average bookstore are any indication, we are, like Paul's Athenian audience, "in every way . . . very religious" (Acts 17:22). But in the schemes of self-help advice God is not worshiped; he is used. This bland "spirituality," no less than atheism, suppresses our knowledge of the God revealed in Scripture.

Captive to sin "in Adam," we are also willing accomplices to our own imprisonment (John 8:44; Rom 5:12). Only when God reaches down and liberates us from this captivity are we truly free to realize our humanity (John 8:36).

A STAY OF EXECUTION

THE STORY MIGHT HAVE ENDED here with humanity trapped under the sentence of death. History would continue as a hopeless cycle of birth and death, culminating in "the lake of fire . . . the second death" (Rev 20:14). Or God could have wiped humanity from the face of the earth and started over. Instead, God follows the death sentence with the surprising announcement of the gospel. Through the offspring of the woman, he promised to crush the serpent's head (Gen 3:15). This is the beginning of a covenant of grace: "The Lord God made garments of skin for Adam and his wife and clothed them" (Gen 3:21). In providing a covering for his rebellious image bearers, we catch a glimpse of God's future plan, "the Lamb of God, who takes away the sin of the world" (John 1:29).

It was a good thing that God did not allow Adam and Eve to eat from the tree of life after they had eaten from the tree of the knowledge of good and evil. To protect them, he exiles the couple from his garden to live "east of Eden," placing cherubim at the gate to bar reentry. The tree of life was the prize of immortality to be eaten if Adam had completed his trial faithfully. Eating from this tree in a state of rebellion would have consigned themselves and all of their posterity—including you and me—to everlasting condemnation. Graciously, God expelled them from Eden with the promise of a coming Savior. Because of this stay of execution, "the promise of entering his rest still stands" (Heb 4:1).

In the next chapter of Genesis, Eve gives birth to a son. She announces at Cain's birth, "With the help of the Lord I have brought forth a man" (Gen 4:1). Eve seems to have thought that she has given birth to the Messiah. But she would soon learn that Cain was not the Messiah. In fact, her firstborn son was the first antichrist.

In the verses that follow, Cain kills his younger brother Abel. Cain was jealous that Abel's animal sacrifice was accepted by God, whereas God "did not look with favor" upon Cain and his offering (Gen 4:5). As heinous as this first murder was, even after the crime God protects Cain. He allows him to build a city and to produce descendants who distinguish themselves as leaders in various cultural endeavors. And right at the point where the genealogy of Cain and the erection of his proud city is recounted (vv. 17–24), we read by contrast that another child was born to Adam and Eve. Eve "named him Seth, saying, 'God has granted me another child in place of Abel, since Cain killed him.' Seth also had a son, and he named him Enosh. At that time people began to call on the name of the Lord" (vv. 25–26).

The stay of execution would continue, as God opens up space within history—now defined by transgression and curse—for the arrival of the promised redeemer and the gathering of a people who call on his name.

CHAPTER 6

GOD MADE A PROMISE

I WAS RAISED IN A CHURCH that loved the Bible. Sunday school was more than just punch and cookies. There were "sword drills" (think of the game show *Jeopardy*, but all about the Bible) where we competed to test our Bible knowledge. Yet with all of this knowledge of the Bible, I never knew how it all fit together. There were lots of interesting (and some not so interesting) stories. But I never heard the big story that moves with dramatic force from Genesis to Revelation. For the most part the Old Testament was alien to me, and I was lost in the forest of its laws and rituals.

HOW DO YOU MAKE SENSE OF THE OLD TESTAMENT?

I N THAT CHURCH during those years, the one thing we could always count on hearing in the teaching from the Old Testament was a character study. We learned that Abraham was the man of faith. Joseph was an awesome example of how to stand against temptation and, if you just wait on the Lord's timing, he will be sure to make your way prosperous as well. Moses is, well, Moses. Joshua's life provides you with leadership tips to be strong and courageous. Then there was Samson—that tough guy who used his muscles for the Lord. David was "a man after God's own heart." One hymn we sang encouraged us to "Dare to Be a Daniel." I learned that the Old Testament was a collection of heroic stories that nevertheless didn't always seem to relate to each other.

Years later, I made the joyful discovery that these Old Testament stories were all connected. Each was a new episode in the unfolding drama of redemption. At the same time, I was surprised to return to these stories and realize that Abraham was capable of lying, scheming, and questioning God's promise. I saw that Moses failed God several times and was barred from entering the promised land. Reading Samson's story, I realized that it was less about "going big for God" than about another cycle of sin, grace, and obedience (repeat). His life was sort of like my own life but without the biceps. And although God called David a man after his own heart (1 Sam 13:14), David was a man of many faults. His selfishness led him to adultery and bloodshed.

If these stories are given to us as moral examples, we might need some new moral examples. They aren't always good ones for us to follow. The good news is that this is not their main purpose. Certainly we can learn from good examples where we find them, but these seemingly unrelated stories are actually episodes in a larger story. Scripture is the epic story of the coming offspring of Abraham through whom the nations would be blessed, of the prophet greater than Moses who leads us to the true promised land, and of the faithful king whom God the Father calls "my Son, whom I love; with him I am well pleased" (Matt 3:17).

Jesus himself told us to read the Bible—which at that point was the Old Testament—with himself as the central character. The religious leaders and scribes loved and studied the Bible diligently, Jesus said, but they did not understand it because they had rejected him. He is the one of whom the scriptures speak (John 5:39). After his resurrection, Jesus met two dejected disciples walking along a road. "He said to them, 'How foolish you are, and how slow to believe all that the prophets have spoken! Did not the Messiah have to suffer these things and then enter his glory?' And beginning with Moses and all the Prophets, he explained to them what was said in all the Scriptures concerning himself" (Luke 24:25–27).

Evidently in those forty days between his resurrection and ascension, Jesus's instruction paid off. The disciples got it. We know this because all of the apostolic sermons in Acts proclaim Christ as the fulfillment of the Old Testament. God is the only real hero in the grand story of judgment and deliverance, and in the letters of the New Testament the apostles unpack this Christ-centered, promise-fulfillment "big story." With its plot and intriguing subplots, this drama gives rise to doctrines that arouse doxology and discipleship, as we follow Christ into the new age he has inaugurated. The Gospels help us to see that Jesus is not only God incarnate. Reading the story of Jesus in light of the Old Testament, we find that he is the faithful prophet, priest, and king that Adam and his posterity—including Israel—failed to be. He fulfilled the commission that God gave to humanity and entered heaven a conqueror with us in his train (Heb 2:10–15)!

The Bible is the history of a very specific promise. It is the unfolding of God's promise that though we deserve nothing but death, God will bring us into his glory through the incarnation, life, death, resurrection, ascension, and return of his Son. In this story, Abraham and Moses and David and Daniel all take their place with us as joyful beneficiaries of the promised gift of eternal life. God is the real hero of the Bible.

THE POWER OF THE PROMISE

PROMISES ARE POWERFUL. I knew an elderly woman who was dying of multiple complications from surgery. On one of my visits, I left her bedside certain that this would be my last. However, that evening she received a call from her son. He promised her that he would catch the next flight from Hong Kong to see her. Amazingly, she remained alive until he arrived. In fact, for the few days of his visit she seemed to be recovering. After he left, she said her good-byes and left this world.

Depending on what is promised and the one who is making it, a promise can have the power to spark hope and life beyond all odds. And God made us such a promise. It's a worldwide, game-changing promise, and every story in the Bible finds its way back to this promise. Yet when we read the Old Testament without understanding how the parts fit together, it all feels rather confusing, like a jigsaw puzzle without the box-top. You have hundreds of these little pieces, but you aren't sure how they all fit together or what pattern they reveal when the puzzle is complete. As you start working on the puzzle, the only way to know the picture is to locate the box-top. What do you see? A portrait of Jesus Christ.

Another helpful way to see how everything fits together is to understand that the Bible is made up of many different genres, or types of writing. Jews, including Jesus and his apostles, would refer to the Old Testament as "the law and the prophets" or "the law, the prophets, and the writings." The Law includes the five books of Moses (also called the Pentateuch). Much of this part of the Bible is historical narrative—reporting how God gave his law and how Israel did in keeping it. Then you have "the writings," a name that is generic enough to include a variety of genres. Among the Writings are wisdom books and a hymnal—the Psalms—for doxology (lament, confession, praise, and worship). Finally you have the prophetic writings. As God's lawyers, they argue the case of "God versus Israel" (Hos 6:7). And yet they also bring a word of hope, of God's promise of life beyond the fall, just as we first heard in Genesis 3:15. The thread that ties it all together is the development of this single promise, repeated in various ways and with slightly different emphases, from Genesis to Revelation. Let's take a closer look at how the promise of Genesis 3:15 unfolds throughout the Old Testament and into the New.

COVENANT: THE CONTEXT OF THE PROMISE

ISRAEL'S PAGAN NEIGHBORS generally believed that they had a *natural* relationship with the gods. In sharp contrast, Israel's relationship with God was *covenantal*. To be related to God covenantally means that he is the Lord and we are his servants. When God sought to establish this sort of relationship with Israel, he chose a political arrangement that was familiar throughout the region and beyond: a treaty.

When a lesser kingdom or city was invaded by enemies, a greater king might come to the rescue. In view of the rescuer's mercy, the lesser kingdom would acknowledge the rescuer as their lord. In many cases, the lord would create a treaty—a covenant—and seal it in a public ceremony by making the lesser king pass through the pieces of severed animals. In doing this, the servant was assuming the same fate as the animals if he should fail to keep the terms of the covenant. The treaty or covenant typically followed a set pattern. It began by identifying the lord who was imposing the covenant and giving the reasons why he should be obeyed as lord. This was followed by various commands, called "stipulations," after which came sanctions, which listed blessings for obedience and curses for disobedience. Finally, a copy of the treaty would be deposited in the shrine of both parties. Henceforth, the lesser kingdom could live in security—but only as long as it was a loyal member of the empire.

God set up a covenant—a treaty—between himself and humanity at creation. When he did this, he issued only one stipulation to Adam that he should not eat of the tree of the knowledge of good and evil. There were also sanctions that accompanied the agreement: life for obedience and death for disobedience. We have already seen what happened—Adam and Eve violated the terms of the covenant. But even after the Lord arraigned Adam and Eve for their transgression, he promised them a seed of the woman who would one day crush the serpent's head (Gen 3:15). This promise began a new stage in history—the war of the seed of the woman and the serpent, who is assisted by a retinue of fallen angels and earthly emissaries.

THE ABRAHAMIC COVENANT

MULTIPLE GENERATIONS pass and human depravity multiplies and spreads across the face of the earth. God wipes the earth clean with the flood, starting afresh with a new family (Noah). God swears never again to bring such a flood. Every time God sees the rainbow in the sky, he will remember his promise to the whole creation. This covenant did not promise redemption from sin, but only a stay of execution. On the basis of this covenant, God commands humanity to "be fruitful and multiply" and to refrain from murder (Gen 9:1–7).

It kept history open to God's plan of redemption. But the cycle of sin continues to spread. Time passes and God calls a man named Abram (later called Abraham) out of a moon-worshiping family and makes a covenant with him (Gen 12–17). In this covenant (especially as related in chapter 15), God promised to give Abraham an inheritance. This would entail an innumerable multitude of physical descendants in their own land as a nation, and an innumerable multitude of spiritual descendants for an everlasting kingdom taken from all the nations of the earth. Abraham believed the promise and was justified through faith, trusting the word that God had spoken. Then, with Abraham asleep, *God himself* passed between the animal pieces. God alone swore the oath and assumed the sanctions.

After several years, God provided Isaac to Abraham and his wife Sarah. But then he tested the patriarch's loyalty by commanding him to sacrifice Isaac, the child of promise. Just as Abraham was about to plunge the knife into his son, God stopped him. In Isaac's place, God provided a ram for the sacrifice.

God's promise to Abraham is passed down from Abraham to Isaac and then again from Isaac to his son Jacob. And in a similar episode in Genesis 28, God reaffirms his oath to Jacob. While he is sleeping, Jacob has a vision of a stairway stretching from heaven to earth with angels ascending and descending upon it. God then reaffirms his pledge to Abraham.

Genesis 37–47 tells the story of Joseph, the eleventh of Jacob's twelve sons. Jealous of Joseph, his brothers sold him into slavery and Joseph ended up in Egypt serving under Potiphar, captain of Pharaoh's guard. Through a series of intriguing twists and turns, Joseph is brought before Pharaoh to interpret his dreams of coming disaster. Pharaoh accepts Joseph's interpretation and advice and makes Joseph prime minister of Egypt. Through a dramatic series of events, Joseph is reunited with his family. They all come to Egypt, where Jacob's descendants multiply rapidly. Even though Joseph was betrayed by his brothers and spent much of his life living in slavery, he forgives his brothers and is used by God to save his family: "You intended to harm me, but God intended it for good to accomplish what is now being done, the saving of many lives" (Gen 50:20).

After Joseph's death, Israel's fortunes turned. "Then a new king, to whom Joseph meant nothing, came to power in Egypt" (Exod 1:8). For the next four centuries, the Hebrews would serve as slaves to the Egyptian rulers.

THE SINAI COVENANT

AT THIS POINT, the story picks up hundreds of years later. After observing the stunning numerical growth of the Hebrews, Pharaoh had all the male Hebrew children thrown into the Nile to drown. However, one mother hid her infant in bulrushes beside the river. Coming to bathe, one of Pharaoh's daughters discovers the infant and raises him as her own child in Pharaoh's court. Moses grows up with wealth and privilege yet rejects it all to lead the Hebrews. Yet he finds himself rejected by them. Alone in the wilderness, he witnesses a bush that burns but is not consumed. From it he hears God calling him to confront Pharaoh—the lord of Egypt—to command him to release the people of Lord Yahweh, so they can freely worship him in the desert. After a series of dramatic miracles and confrontations that demonstrate the power of Yahweh over the gods of Egypt, the people depart Egypt. On the night of their deliverance, God's judgment falls on Egypt. Every firstborn—whether human or animal—is killed by the angel of God's wrath except those among the Israelites who have brushed their doors with the blood of a young lamb. God's judgment "passes over" those who are covered in the blood. Eventually the people escape the power of Pharaoh through a parting of the waters of the Red Sea by God's "outstretched arm" (Exod 6:6).

Moses leads the people to Mount Sinai where God delivers the law to Moses as the mediator of a covenant with the nation. Besides the Ten Commandments, God delivers detailed commands governing every aspect of Israel's life in the land that he was giving them. Along with the bloody sacrifices, the tabernacle and its priesthood testified to the seriousness of sin, the danger of God's holiness, and the need for a mediator greater than Moses to reconcile us to God.

The Holy Spirit continued to lead the people on their route toward the promised land with a cloud by day and a glowing pillar at night. Whenever the cloud moved, the priests pulled up the stakes of the tabernacle and the twelve tribes set out again for another leg of the journey. Sadly, however, this was not Israel's finest hour. Like children on a family vacation, they were often impatient and selfish, asking, "Are we there yet?" Soon their private grumbling became public quarreling and open rebellion. Had they forgotten God's mighty acts of liberation from Egypt? No, but they longed for the pleasures of Egypt where they'd had water and food rations. They soon forgot the misery of their enslavement and were no longer grateful for the Lord's mighty acts of liberation from Egypt. Their quarrelling and grumbling against Moses was actually an attack on God's leadership and plan as well as his goodness and power.

Yet God remained faithful to his people. He told Moses to strike a rock and when he did, water gushed out like a fountain. At one point when the Israelites rebelled again and put Moses on trial, threatening him with death, God told Moses:

"Go out in front of the people. Take with you some of the elders of Israel and take in your hand the staff with which you struck the Nile, and go. I will stand there before you by the rock at Horeb. Strike the rock, and water will come out of it for the people to drink." So Moses did this in the sight of the elders of Israel. And he called the place Massah ["testing"] and Meribah ["quarreling"] because the Israelites quarreled and because they tested the Lord saying, "Is the Lord among us or not?" (Exod 17:5–7)

A careful reading of this passage reveals that it is a courtroom scene. The people are putting Moses on trial but Moses is only the mediator. Ultimately the people are rebelling against God's leadership. They are charging God with criminal negligence. Yet instead of destroying them on the spot as he had every right to do, God mercifully assumes the place of a defendant. "I will stand there *before you* by the rock," God said, thus allowing himself to be struck by his own staff for the people's benefit. The righteous Lord and Judge takes the position of the accused and is struck to save his unrighteous accusers.

Yet there were consequences for their disobedience and grumbling. The Lord did not let this faithless generation enter Canaan to possess the promised land. Moses himself died having only viewed it from the mountain. Instead, his lieutenant Joshua led the people into the land that God had promised to Abraham's descendants in Genesis 15. The book of Joshua records the march of Lord Yahweh through the land to cleanse and give it to his people as he promised. Israel was called to cleanse the land; however, it was God himself who carried it out.

A key point we should note in the story is that the land was God's. The land did not belong to Israel any more than it belonged to the Canaanites, Hittites, or Amorites. In fact, if Israel broke covenant with God, he promised to drive them out as well. Israel crossed the Jordan and began its conquest. Yet throughout these episodes of holy war, it is clear that God was the one conquering and delivering his enemies into Israel's hand.

After God divided and distributed the conquered land among the twelve tribes, Joshua reminded the people of the covenant that God had made with Abraham: "You know with all your heart and soul that not one of all the good promises the Lord your God gave you has failed. Every promise has been fulfilled; not one has failed" (Josh 23:14).

We pause here because this was an important announcement. Note carefully that Joshua emphasizes the *complete fulfillment* of the land promise. Yet recall that at Mount Sinai, the people had sworn allegiance and assumed full responsibility for the terms of this covenant. In fact, Joshua reminded them that there would be severe consequences for breaking the covenant: "[The Lord] will bring on you all the evil things he has threatened, until the Lord your God has destroyed you from this good land he has given you. If you violate the covenant of the Lord your God . . . you will quickly perish from the good land he has given you" (Josh 23:15b–16).

Though the people quickly renewed their allegiance to the Sinai covenant, Joshua knew that their eagerness would be short lived: "Joshua said to the people, 'You are not able to serve the Lord. He is a holy God; he is a jealous God. He will not forgive your rebellion and your sins'" (Josh 24:19). This wasn't exactly an inspirational pep talk! Again note that there is nothing in the Sinai covenant that obligated the Lord. The covenant at Sinai contained no promise obligating God; instead the commands were to be fulfilled by Israel and the sanctions of blessing or curse depended on the nation's obedience. The Sinai covenant was a precarious covenant, based upon the loyalty of sinners. Joshua's warning was prophetic.

We see why as we enter the book of Judges and pick up the story again. As soon as Joshua died, "the Israelites did evil in the eyes of the

Lord and served the Baals. They forsook the Lord, the God of their ancestors, who had brought them out of Egypt. . . . Then the Lord raised up judges, who saved them out of the hands of these raiders. Yet they would not listen to their judges but prostituted themselves to other gods and worshiped them" (Judg 2:11–12, 16–17). Sometimes the people would follow a judge, but after one died the people returned to their rebellious ways. Again we see the drama replayed. The serpent—that is, the remaining idolaters left in Israel—drew each new generation away from the Lord. Like Adam, Israel refused to cleanse God's land and themselves from idolatry.

God raises up a final judge named Samuel, who is God's faithful prophet. Samuel called Israel to put away the foreign gods and return to God as their king. He told the people that if they would renew their loyalty to the God of Sinai, then God would deliver them from the hand of the Philistines. The people listened to Samuel and obeyed the Lord.

In his old age Samuel made his sons judges over Israel. But they were corrupt men, taking bribes and perverting justice (1 Sam 8:3). Instead of more judges, Israel wanted something more permanent: "a king . . . such as all the other nations have"—a king they could see (1 Sam 8:5). Samuel was dismayed with this plea, but God told him to allow it because "it is not you they have rejected, but they have rejected me as their king" (v. 7). Isn't it amazing that God mercifully allowed this demand and continued to work graciously among his rebellious people?

THE DAVIDIC COVENANT

THE FIRST KING chosen by God was a man named Saul, but after he offered an unlawful sacrifice his heart turned from the Lord. The Lord rejected Saul as king, anointing the shepherd-boy David in his place as the next king of Israel (1 Sam 13–16). The Holy Spirit, now absent from Saul, rushed upon David as he slew the giant Goliath. But David is not the hero in this story. David wanted everyone to recognize the real hero. So he responded to Goliath's boasting by stating that God would act to defeat the giant, so that "the whole world will know that there is a God in Israel. All those gathered here will know that it is not by sword or spear that the Lord saves; for the battle is the Lord's, and he will give all of you into our hands" (1 Sam 17:46–47). Despite the nation's decision, David believed that God was still Israel's true king.

David eventually replaced Saul as king and later in his life wanted to build a temple for God. It was an understandable desire. The era of God's moving presence, leading his people from a portable tent called the tabernacle, was over. The people were established in the land and God had already delivered to Moses the temple's design. All that remained was for the temple to be built. Each detail of the design served collectively to point to "the Lamb of God, who takes away the sin of the world" (John 1:29). The details of the temple and the service of the priests communicated that there was a way in which God could be forever present among his people in peace rather than judgment.

God would allow David's son to build the temple. But he had something far greater in mind with this promise. God would not allow David to serve him by building a physical structure: "Are you the one to build me a house to dwell in? I have not dwelt in a house from the day I brought the Israelites up out of Egypt to this day. I have been moving from place to place with a tent as my dwelling" (2 Sam 7:5–6). Instead, God served David with a promise: "The Lord himself will establish a house for you" (v. 11). He continues:

> When your days are over and you rest with your ancestors, I will raise up your offspring to succeed you, your own flesh and blood, and I will establish his kingdom. He [i.e., Solomon] is the one who

*will build a house for my Name, and I will establish the throne
of his kingdom forever. I will be his father, and he will be my son.
When he does wrong, I will punish him with a rod wielded by
men, with floggings inflicted by human hands. But my love will
never be taken away from him, as I took it away from Saul, whom
I removed from before you. Your house and your kingdom will
endure forever before me; your throne will be established forever.
(2 Sam 7:12–16)*

Like all of us, David was a sinful man, and he indulged his sinful
heart. His reign was besotted by episodes of violence. Once, demanding
the woman he craved sexually, he seduced her and sent her husband into
battle to die. His family life was broken by violence and discord. His
eldest son Absalom killed his own half brother and attempted a coup,
but the conspiracy was put down and Absalom was killed. David's house
was a mess, and yet God again was gracious. Like the promise made to
Abraham, God's oath to David was unbreakable. The development of
God's promise to Abraham was now continuing through the office of
the king, the representative head of the Lord's people. God indicated
that the house of David would have an everlasting throne. David's last
words extol the Lord's promise: "If my house were not right with God,
surely he would not have made with me an everlasting covenant, ar-
ranged and secured in every part" (2 Sam 23:5).

Although the reign of David's son Solomon began well, his heart
turned from the Lord as he followed after his many foreign wives.
Solomon welcomed idolatrous shrines and festivals as well. God raised
up the rod of men to discipline Solomon—various rulers and leaders of
rogue bands—even as he continued to keep his promise to David.

Under Solomon's foolish and oppressive son Rehoboam, the nation
divided. "Only the tribe of Judah remained loyal to the house of David"

(1 Kgs 12:20). The people were split, with Israel in the north and Judah in the south. Sadly, as the story unfolds, we meet no king in the years that follow who is quite like David. In most cases, the record shows no loyalty to the Lord. With some kings, their devotion to God is mixed. Only in a few instances do we find kings with a heart wholly for the Lord. Again, we are reminded that it is God's promise that keeps the story moving forward, not the faithfulness of the kings. As the generations pass, there nevertheless remains a Davidic heir on the throne.

One of the kings of Israel, Ahab, marries a non-Israelite, Jezebel, who convinces him to bring back Baal worship, the worship of a false god: "Ahab . . . did more to arouse the anger of the Lord, the God of Israel, than did all the kings of Israel before him" (1 Kgs 16:33). His wife Jezebel's ruthlessness knew no bounds. The serpent—the enemy of God and his people—now had his own king and queen upon the throne of Israel. Yet there was still a man of God for the nation—a prophet named Elijah. In a power confrontation on a mountaintop, Elijah triumphs over the prophets of Baal and prophesies the death of Ahab. After Ahab's death, Jezebel remains a powerful foe, seeking to destroy the seed of David in Judah by slaughter.

One bright spot during these troubled times was the zealous campaign of King Jehu of Israel, who tried to wipe out Baal worship from the land. Jehu killed the prophets of Baal, had the altars and shrines destroyed, and had Jezebel executed. And yet in the end, Jehu too fell into the sins of his fathers (2 Kgs 10:18–36).

If we step back from the drama for a moment, we see that God's ancient enemy, the serpent, was at work in all of this, trying to intercept the line of David to wipe out God's promised king. We see this war between the "seed of the woman" and the serpent (Gen 3:15) quite clearly in the reign of Athaliah over Judah. When her son King Ahaziah died, "she proceeded to destroy the whole royal family" (2 Kgs 11:1). If she had succeeded, this would have meant the end of God's promise to have a Davidic heir on the throne.

> But Jehosheba, the daughter of King Jehoram and sister of Ahaziah, took Joash son of Ahaziah and stole him away from among the royal princes, who were about to be murdered. She put him and his nurse in a bedroom to hide him from Athaliah; so he was not killed. He remained hidden with his nurse at the temple of the Lord for six years while Athaliah ruled the land. (2 Kgs 11:2–3)

Jehoiada, the high priest at the time, gathered the captains of the Carites—Israel's secret service. Showing them the royal boy, he designed a plot to arrest Queen Athaliah and the plan succeeded. The priest and captains brought Joash out to the people and placed the crown on his head and anointed him, and the people "clapped their hands and shouted, 'Long live the king!'" (2 Kgs 11:5–12). Queen Athaliah was executed and "all the people of the land went to the temple of Baal and tore it down. They smashed the altars and idols to pieces and killed Mattan the priest of Baal in front of the altars" (v. 18). At just seven years of age, Joash began his reign, repairing the temple of the Lord and destroying the temples of Baal. "The high places, however, were not removed; the people continued to offer sacrifices and burn incense there" (2 Kgs 12:3).

What do we learn from all of this? First, God kept his promise to Adam and Eve, Abraham, and David. The serpent did not intercept the promised Son. Second, even with the best of kings, there is always a "nevertheless." The recurring question throughout these stories is this: When will there be a righteous king who reunites Israel and Judah and reigns as God's own emissary?

COVENANT CURSES AND FUTURE BLESSINGS

G OD'S JUDGMENT eventually fell upon Israel and the people were sent into exile by the Assyrians. Then, several generations afterward, a similar fate befell Judah and the people were sent into Babylonian captivity. The part of the Bible called "the Prophets" spans the period from just before the exile to just after exiles were released to return to Israel and rebuild the temple.

Who were these prophets? As I mentioned earlier, they were God's covenant attorneys, bringing his lawsuit against Israel and Judah. On the basis of the Sinai covenant, the prophets pressed the charges and announced the sanctions: death, destruction, and exile from God's land. The "glory of the Lord" departed the temple (Ezek 10:18). God's earthly residence was no longer the temple mount. Yet along with accusation, God also comforted the exiles with prophesies of a hope beyond their captivity. On the basis of the Sinai covenant, Israel no longer had a claim to the land. The land and the temple had both been desecrated—not by pagans but by the people of God. Yet hope remained, not in the Sinai covenant, but on the basis of the Abrahamic and Davidic covenants. These covenants held the promise of a new future for God's people.

Earlier, we saw in the trial of Adam and Eve that their sentencing was followed by a surprising and glorious announcement of the gospel. A redeemer would arise who would crush the serpent's head (Gen 3:15). This same pattern is now repeated with the prophets. After God arraigns his people and issues his sentence upon them, he promises "a new covenant" (Jer 31:31–34). This covenant would "not be like the covenant I made with their ancestors" at Mount Sinai, "'because they broke my covenant, though I was a husband to them,' declares the Lord" (v. 32). The new covenant would be different from the Sinai covenant, which was conditional and based upon the obedience of the people. Instead, this pledge, like the ones God had made to Adam and Eve, to Abraham and Sarah, and to David, transcended the infidelity of the people. Its fulfillment depended not on the people, but on God.

The people's unfaithfulness brought redemptive history to a standstill. Yet God's faithfulness pushed history forward toward its fulfillment in Jesus Christ. In its deepest, darkest, and most hopeless days of exile, Israel heard God vow, "You will be my people, and I will be your God" (Jer 30:22).

The prophets continually return to this promise of one who will rule on David's throne forever in righteousness, blessing, and peace (Isa 9:6–7). He would be the prophet greater than Moses. He would be the greater Joshua who would cleanse the whole earth and give his people rest on every side. He would be the good shepherd who gathers his holy nation from a remnant of Israel and the nations (Jer 3:15–17, with John 10:11). He would be the Son of Man—a clearly divine as well as human figure from the book of Daniel (Dan 7:13–14). The boundaries that defined the nation of Israel would be expanded beyond their wildest dreams, and the Lord would remove the death shroud that lay over the world (Isa 25:7–8). There would be feasting with God forever (Isa 25:6).

Something lay ahead that was far greater than the exodus from Egypt and the glorious days of the conquest of the promised land. It was something far greater than a renewal of the Sinai covenant, with a geopolitical theocracy. This was not a conditional and temporary covenant promising "long life" in a parcel of real estate in the ancient Near East. It was a new covenant, a far greater covenant, with greater promises and a greater mediator.

Adam, Israel, and—in Adam, all of us—have failed to keep our promise to God. Yet God's promise remains. It is to the fulfillment of that promise that we turn next.

CHAPTER 7

JOY TO THE WORLD!

CHRISTMAS JUST WOULDN'T BE CHRISTMAS without songs, but in an effort to avoid the explicitly Christian roots of the season, many of today's songs are sentimental. Since I grew up in California, I can't relate to chestnuts roasting on an open fire or Jack Frost nipping at my nose—at Christmas or any other time. These generic "holiday" songs have more to do with nostalgic memories of childhood than with a Jewish Messiah born two millennia ago.

Yet they illustrate a sad truth. A world crazy for happiness cannot lift its gaze above the trivial. Rather than look for our happiness in sentimentalized memories of the not-too-distant past, it is the real Christmas story that has generated centuries of *joy*—a profound kind of pleasure that the world can imitate but never reproduce. If the drama of the Bible, the story we unfolded in the previous chapter, gives rise to a specific set of doctrines (our understanding of God and his activity), it also shapes our doxology. This refers to the way we experience and express for ourselves the wonder of God's having made us part of his story in Jesus Christ.

Here I want to pick up where we left off—the meaning of Jesus within the Bible's story of Israel and the world. It is important to see Jesus's identity not only from the *doctrine* as it's mined from individual Old Testament texts, but to see it in light of the flow of Israel's story that is the *drama* of salvation, and the *doxologies* it provokes. Only then will we understand how our *discipleship* flows from that.

ADVENT

WHEN YOU HEAR the best news in the world, the only appropriate response is to sing. And that is precisely what Mary did when the angel Gabriel announced to her that she would conceive God himself by the power of the Holy Spirit. What was her response? At first she was astonished: "How will this be . . . since I am a virgin?" (Luke 1:34). "The angel answered, 'The Holy Spirit will come on you, and the power of the Most High will overshadow you. So the holy one to be born will be called the Son of God'" (v. 35). Trusting the promise, Mary replied, "I am the Lord's servant. . . . May your word to me be fulfilled" (v. 38). Then Mary composed a new song from various passages of the Old Testament, drawing especially from the Psalms:

> *My soul glorifies the Lord*
> *and my spirit rejoices in God my Savior,*
> *for he has been mindful of the humble state of his servant.*
> *From now on all generations will call me blessed,*
> *for the Mighty One has done great things for me—*
> *holy is his name.*

His mercy extends to those who fear him,
    from generation to generation.
He has performed mighty deeds with his arm;
    he has scattered those who are proud in their inmost thoughts.
He has brought down rulers from their thrones
    but has lifted up the humble.
He has filled the hungry with good things
    but has sent the rich away empty.
He has helped his servant Israel,
    remembering to be merciful
to Abraham and his descendents forever,
    just as he promised our ancestors. (vv. 46–55)

As we have seen, one way of summarizing the Bible's big plot is by seeing it as a war between the serpent and the seed of the woman. Satan knows that God works within history. He knows that God has tied the fulfillment of his promise to a particular person from a particular line of Jewish kings. This person must not only be the seed of the woman but also the seed of Abraham and Sarah. Moreover, he must be from the tribe of Judah, the seed of King David. So Satan sets his eyes on intercepting this messianic seed at various points along that family line.

When we arrive at the birth of Jesus Christ, we see the satanic strategy of eliminating the promised seed at work once again. Even as the angels sing to celebrate his birth, the demons come out of the woodwork to subvert the Messiah's undoing of their kingdom. The battle is on between the serpent and the seed of the woman.

As in the days of Pharaoh who massacred the male infants of the Hebrews, Herod attempts to massacre the same of Bethlehem where Jesus is born. Ironically, God delivers his son—with Joseph and his mother Mary—by telling them to flee to Egypt. When Jesus returns with his family to settle in the town of Nazareth, it was like another exodus, fulfilling the prophecy of Hosea 11:1, "Out of Egypt I called my son" (see Matt 2:15).

Revelation 12 offers us a vivid snapshot of the events between Christ's first coming as an infant and his future coming as judge and king. The author describes a woman. She is clothed with the sun, with the moon under her feet, wearing a crown of twelve stars. This woman symbolically represents the church in the Old Testament. She signifies Israel from whom the Savior would come. The woman is in the pains of childbirth with the dragon—Satan—waiting to devour the child (vv. 1–4). There is perhaps no better picture of the war of the serpent and the seed of the woman in all of the Bible. The baby is born "a male child, who 'will rule all the nations with an iron scepter'" (v. 5, quoting Ps 2:9). Furthermore, "her child was snatched up to God and to his throne. The woman fled into the wilderness to a place prepared for her by God, where she might be taken care of for 1,260 days" (vv. 5–6). While all interpreters believe that this number is symbolic, most throughout church history have taken it to refer to the period in which we are now living, the period between Christ's ascension and his future return.

Beginning with verse 7, we have another snapshot of this same reality. A heavenly war breaks out, with Michael the archangel defeating the dragon—Satan—and casting him out of heaven. The "ancient serpent . . . who leads the whole world astray. . . . was hurled to the earth, and his angels with him" (v. 9). These fallen angels swarmed around Jesus and possessed those he came to liberate. In fact, we see this when we read the Gospels. Jesus begins his ministry by overcoming Satan's temptation in sharp contrast with the trial of Adam in the garden of Eden and Israel in the wilderness.

The conclusion becomes clear. Jesus has won the war. Satan's kingdom has been decisively conquered. Yet there are still skirmishes to be fought. The coheirs of Christ, his church, can now loot Satan's palace and liberate his dungeons. Satan is bound so that he can no longer deceive the nations, and the gospel can have success in the power of the Spirit. This does not mean that Satan is powerless. He can still stir up troubles and persecutions, and even take lives through martyrdom. Yet despite these trials—and in fact, through them—the gospel is spreading. Christ's kingdom even now is triumphing through "the blood of the Lamb and by the word of their testimony" (v. 11).

Having failed to destroy the Messiah, Satan "pursued the woman who had given birth to the male child" (v. 13). But the church was given wings to fly into the wilderness for these 1,260 days—again, a reference to the era in which we now live. After this period of blessing upon the gospel through suffering and testimony, "the dragon was enraged at the woman and went off to wage war against the rest of her offspring—those who keep God's commands and hold fast their testimony about Jesus" (v. 17).

So a battle still rages even though the war has been decisively won already by Christ. In fact, Satan's rage against the church is aroused by the fact that "he knows that his time is short" (v. 12).

THE TRUE AND FAITHFUL SON

MATTHEW'S GOSPEL OPENS with the genealogy of Jesus. In fact, his Gospel is the book of "the genealogy of Jesus the Messiah the son of David, the son of Abraham" (Matt 1:1). Luke's Gospel traces this same genealogy from Jesus back to "Adam, the son of God" (Luke 3:38). This is no small matter, since God has indeed bound up his promise with the real events of history. More specifically, he has bound up our salvation with a very particular line descended from Adam through Abraham and the lineage of David.

At the time of Jesus's birth, the Roman Empire under Caesar Augustus was Israel's master, and Herod the Great was the puppet king of the Jews. Herod's ancestry was Arab and Edomite and his parents had converted to Judaism. So Herod was not a royal son of David, though he tried to forge this ancestry. Everyone knew it was a joke—and a cruel one—since he was a murderous thug with an ambitious building program. And everyone knew that "theocracy"—that is, a kingdom where God alone is king—was a distant memory, recalled now only through written texts. From the Babylonians to the Romans, Israel was an occupied land. The Spirit of God had not spoken for four centuries.

It is this background that we should bear in mind as we encounter "Son of God" as one of Jesus's titles. It is important that we define his titles according to the way that they are used throughout the Bible's story. The Scriptures speak of Adam as a "son" of God, an image bearer created to faithfully represent God. There is also a great deal of biblical evidence that refers to Israel as an adopted "son of God." After Moses told God that he didn't like the plan for getting the people out of Egypt, God replied, "Then say to Pharaoh, 'This is what the Lord says: Israel is *my firstborn son*, and I told you, "Let my son go, so he may worship me." But you refused to let him go; so I will kill *your* firstborn son'" (Exod 4:22–23; emphasis added). We know what happened. Pharaoh did not let God's people go. And God did destroy Egypt's firstborn, just as Pharaoh had massacred the Hebrew children.

My children bear my surname. Similarly, to be God's "firstborn son" is to be called by his name (see, e.g., Deut 28:10; 2 Chron 7:14). Yet many of the references to Israel as God's son are not positive. They are frequently made in the context of Israel's forgetfulness and transgression of the covenant. "I reared children and brought them up, but they have rebelled against me (Isa 1:2).

So when it comes to the title "Son of God," uppermost in the Bible's story is the idea of a true and faithful servant who will do everything that the Father has told him to do. It is a title of intimacy. It is also a title of office. We hold our leaders to a higher standard when they break their oaths in scandals and corruption. It is precisely because they hold a trusted office that their infidelity stings so keenly. The tragedy of sin is not that animals like us have behaved as animals; it is that sons of God—the Bible includes males and females under this title—have become like the beasts.

What God is waiting for is a faithful son who will say and do what pleases him—not simply out of duty, but out of the pleasure of offering up to the Father a thankful life that fulfills the purpose of our creation.

Jesus is precisely this unique and faithful son. Fully human, from the line of Jesse, his love for the Father contrasts sharply with the history of the kings who descended from David's father. It is crucial that the Savior of Adam's descendants be fully human. He had to be a son of Adam in order to fulfill the trial that Adam failed and win for us the right to eat from the tree of life. He had to be Abraham's seed by his wife Sarah—the child of promise—rather than by Hagar, the child of human effort. He had to be the son of David to rule upon the everlasting throne.

Jesus is therefore doubly the Son of God. He is God's Son *by nature as the eternally begotten person of the Trinity,* but he is also God's son *by adoption* in the sense that he is the human representative, the *servant of the covenant who finally hears and obeys* every word that the Father speaks. Jesus is the faithful son anticipated in Psalm 2. In that song, the kings of the earth are represented as plotting in vain "against the Lord and against his anointed [Messiah], saying, 'Let us break their chains and throw off their shackles'" (vv. 2–3). God in heaven laughs at these silly maneuvers.

Jesus is the last Adam, the true Israel, the finally faithful son of David. He is "my servant, whom I uphold, my chosen one in whom I delight; I will put my Spirit on him, and he will bring justice to the nations" (Isa 42:1). He will bring mercy, righteousness, and the word of God to the ends of the earth (v. 4).

The Father has always had the Son of his love at his side. He "so loved the world that he gave his one and only Son" (John 3:16). Yet now for the first time in history, he has a faithful *human* son, Jesus of Nazareth, who refused to satisfy his selfish cravings but instead said, "My food . . . is to do the will of him who sent me and to finish his work" (John 4:34).

THE SEED OF ABRAHAM AND SARAH

JESUS IS THE HEIR promised to Abraham through whom "all peoples on earth will be blessed" (Gen 12:3). In Genesis 12, God had promised Abraham innumerable physical *seeds* (plural)—offspring—in a particular land, as well as a *seed* (singular) in whom the nations would be blessed. The land promise was fulfilled when God defeated his enemies and distributed the land of Canaan, the promised land, to the twelve tribes (Josh 21:44–45). But the singular-seed promise was fulfilled and is being fulfilled as the gospel goes out to the nations.

God promised Abraham that Sarah his wife despite her old age would be the mother of promise. God loves working with *nothing*. Just think of how he created everything out of nothing in the beginning. He even loves working with *opposition*. It proves that God alone deserves the glory. Abraham and Sarah did, in fact, provide obstacles: they agreed to try for a child through Hagar the servant. God gave Hagar and her son Ishmael gracious parting gifts. However, Ishmael was not the promised son. Their scheming accomplished nothing, except for an age-old hostility of Ishmael's descendants toward Israel that dominates the daily headlines to the present day.

It is much easier to do something, to take matters into your own hands, than to just sit there and believe a promise that someone else makes about what he'll do. But faith—that is, trust in God's promise—is what God commands and gives by grace. God kept preaching his promise into Abraham's very bones until he and Sarah believed it. He "believed the Lord, and he credited it to him as righteousness" (Gen 15:6).

We already saw how God tested Abraham's trust by commanding him to sacrifice his son:

> *Abraham looked up and there in a thicket he saw a ram caught by its horns. He went over and took the ram and sacrificed it as a burnt offering instead of his son. So Abraham called that place The Lord Will Provide. And to this day it is said, "On the mountain of the Lord it will be provided." (Gen 22:13–14)*

There are at least three amazing things in this passage. First, there is the miracle of Abraham's faith. He trusted that God had a purpose and did not hold back that which God had given him, even his only son. Second, unlike Abraham, who did not need to follow through on the sacrifice of his only son, the Father did give his only Son over to death for our sins. Jesus is not so much anticipated here by Isaac as much as by the ram that is sacrificed in Isaac's place. Third, we should also note the location of the sacrifice: "And to this day it is said, 'On the mountain of the Lord it will be provided.'" This mountain was no less than the future location of the Jerusalem temple. The mount where God called Abraham to sacrifice his only son was the very location where God's Son would be sacrificed centuries later. The promise of a substitute is wrapped in the swaddling clothes of amazingly rich symbolism, though the prophet himself could only imagine what its fulfillment might look like.

You and I can do all sorts of things to try to win God's approval, but this is not the same as standing on his promise. Our works would not be the fruit of trust in God, but the very opposite: arrogant and foolish trust in our own ability to get things done. This is one of the major themes in the background of Abraham's story, and it is what the story of Abraham's greater son—Jesus—is all about. Though Abraham does begin by scheming and striving to obtain a son his own way, he finally rests from his striving and believes God's promise. In this regard, the Bible refers to Abraham as the "father" of all those who believe in God's promises. Those who believe become his spiritual children, his offspring.

To see this, we must fast-forward to the time of John the Baptist. A crowd of people are coming to receive baptism by John for repentance. Even some of the Pharisees and Sadducees showed up, and these folks did not usually appear in public at the same events. John was not very seeker sensitive and when he saw them, he called them out on the spot:

> You brood of vipers! Who warned you to flee from the coming wrath? Produce fruit in keeping with repentance. And do not think you can say to yourselves, "We have Abraham as our father." I tell you that out of these stones God can raise up children for Abraham. (Matt 3:7–9)

Think about how shocking this message would have been. Here we have physical descendants of Abraham—Jewish religious leaders, no less—and John is telling them that they should not presume to think that they are children of Abraham. In other words, John was saying that physical descent no longer counted for anything as far as entering the kingdom of God.

Recall that God had sworn to Abraham a greater reality than having physical descendants in the land of Canaan. God promised him that through his seed—one particular descendant—all the families of the earth would be blessed. That time had come. Jesus was that seed.

It wasn't that the requirements for being a child of Abraham had changed. Even in the Old Testament, inclusion in the Abrahamic promise of a heavenly inheritance is determined by faith in Christ. Here is how the apostle Paul puts the matter:

The promises were spoken to Abraham and to his seed. Scripture does not say "and to seeds," meaning many people, but "and to your seed," meaning one person, who is Christ. What I mean is this: The law, introduced 430 years later, does not set aside the covenant previously established by God and thus do away with the promise. For if the inheritance depends on the law, then it no longer depends on the promise; but God in his grace gave it to Abraham through a promise. (Gal 3:16–18)

In other words, those who would inherit the promises God made to Abraham were not those who kept the Sinai covenant. They are promises made concerning a single individual—Jesus Christ.

THE HEART OF THE GOSPEL

JESUS IS THE FULFILLMENT of everything to which the law pointed. The law—the Sinai covenant—could not annul the Abrahamic promise. We can be justified—declared righteous before God—and made children of Abraham only through faith in Christ, the "seed" in whom the nations would be blessed.

Since God's promise to Abraham pertained to a single individual, namely Christ, how does it become ours? The answer is that we must be in relationship or union with Christ, or as the Bible says, we must be *in* Christ. Christ is our treasure, our refuge from the coming judgment, the source of every spiritual blessing (Eph 1:3–14). *In Christ* we have everything. *Outside of Christ* we have nothing but condemnation. We are chosen, justified, sanctified, and glorified in Christ alone, by grace alone, through faith alone, on the basis of a promise alone—apart from the law. God declares unrighteous people to be righteous even while they are still unrighteous in themselves because they are now in union with Christ.

Folks, this is good news. It is the heart of the gospel. I know that it sounds impossible. How could a just God regard someone as righteous who is actually unrighteous? But as Paul makes clear, it is because Christ gives us his righteousness as a gift. How can he do this? How can a judge simply declare a criminal to be a law-abiding citizen? It's not arbitrary. Jesus lived a perfect life, fulfilling God's law. But he did not just do this for himself. He is our representative, just as Adam was in the garden. Even Adam is "in Christ" through faith in the promise that God gave to him and to Eve in Genesis 3:15. However, all of us are born into this world "in Adam" in the sense that both his guilt and his corruption are passed down to us all. When the Holy Spirit brings us to Christ through the gospel, we are united to Christ. His righteousness becomes truly ours because he has imputed or credited it to us. And our curse is imputed to him. It's a transfer, what the church fathers called "the marvelous exchange." It is our

THE LAW AND THE GOSPEL

God speaks in two words: the law and the gospel. There is a danger in either confusing or separating them. The law commands and the gospel gives. The law says, "Do," and the gospel says, "Done!" Both are good, but God does different things through them.

The law is everything in Scripture that God commands. The gospel is everything in Scripture that makes promises based solely on God's grace to us in Christ. When it comes to how we receive the promises, law and gospel are opposed, for we are saved apart from the law. The law condemns us, while the gospel is the good news that announces our justification that we are free for the first time to embrace God as our Father rather than our Judge. Lutheran and Reformed traditions distinguish three uses of the law: to expose our guilt and drive us to Christ, a civil use to restrain evil, and to guide Christian obedience. More generally, the New Testament frequently employs the terms law and gospel to refer to the old covenant distinguished from the new.

rags for Christ's riches. This is the doctrine of *justification*. Merely human mediators have fallen short. They too are not only unable to save sinners but are sinners themselves. As a nation, Israel was in covenant with God through the mediation of Moses. "But in fact the ministry Jesus has received is as superior to theirs as the covenant of which he is mediator is superior to the old one, since the new covenant is established on better promises" (Heb 8:6). Jesus Christ as God and man has accomplished everything for our salvation. And even now in heaven he continues as our mediator, interceding for us in our weakness. Because he *is* our righteousness (1 Cor 1:30), we stand not only acquitted of our guilt but righteous before God. He is the head and mediator of the covenant of grace. To be united to him is to be justified, gradually sanctified, and finally glorified when he returns.

Sometimes we hear justification defined as "just-as-if-I'd-never-sinned." Yet that's only half the story. It is great news that we are forgiven, but God requires a positive righteousness, not just a lack of violations. He looks upon believers not only as if they had never sinned but as if they had loved him and their neighbors from the heart every moment of our lives. When we place our trust in Christ alone, all our sins are credited to him, and his obedience to all that God commanded is credited to us.

Justification is precisely what we need. To justify means to *declare* righteous. It does not mean to *make* righteous (that is *sanctification*). The law given at Mount Sinai cannot justify anyone.

 JUSTIFICATION AND SANCTIFICATION

Justification and sanctification are both gifts of God given to us in union with Christ. By faith we embrace Christ for the imputation of righteousness (*justification*), a legal verdict by which God declares us "not guilty." By that same faith we are gradually conformed to the likeness of Christ (*sanctification*) as the Spirit works in us to bring forth good works.

Furthermore, it cannot bring God's promised blessing of salvation to all the nations of the earth. In fact, it is precisely this law that keeps Israel separate from the nations. After being fulfilled by the true and faithful Israelite, the old covenant—which Israel did not keep—must come to an end. It must make way for the greater promises of the Abrahamic covenant to be fulfilled in the new covenant.

 ## THE GREATER JOSEPH

You may recall that the patriarch Joseph was favored by God as well as by his own father Jacob. In jealousy Joseph's brothers tore off Joseph's robe and threw him into a pit. But he was raised to life and his brothers later bowed down to him out of gratitude for his mercy. Joseph said to them at that time, "You intended to harm me, but God intended it for good to accomplish what is now being done, the saving of many lives" (Gen 50:20). Jesus is the greater Joseph, favored by his Father above all others. Like Joseph, he was hated by his own brothers, who were jealous of his position—especially his claim to be equal with God. He too was stripped of his robe and thrown into a pit. But he was raised and exalted above every name that can be named (Eph 1:21). There is no name above that of Yahweh, the God of Israel, but Jesus has been given precisely this superlative name.

Throughout his ministry, Jesus was constantly pointing out the difference between those "who were confident of their own righteousness" and those who cried out, like the tax collector, "God, have mercy on me, a sinner" (Luke 18:9, 13). Concerning these two types of people, Jesus said, "I tell you that this man [the tax collector], rather than the other, went home justified before God" (18:14).

When the religious leaders asked him why he dined with sinners, Jesus answered, "It is not the healthy who need a doctor, but the sick. I have not come to call the righteous, but sinners to repentance" (Luke 5:31–32). And, "the Son of Man came to seek and to save the lost" (Luke 19:10). Jesus was issuing a direct challenge to the self-righteous. He was saying that to be part of his kingdom, you must first qualify as a sick sinner.

For the most part, the religious leaders were not willing to see themselves that way. The "sinners" were always someone else. But Jesus was turning the tables.

CHAPTER 8

JESUS IS LORD

I OFTEN MEET PEOPLE who say that they were raised in church but no longer believe in Christ. In many of these cases, something happened—usually a personal tragedy—that disillusioned them. In other cases, the reasons are more global: "I thought he came to make the world a better place. But take a look. The world is a mess." There is a certain danger in trying to gain converts—and keep them—by promising Jesus as the answer to all sorts of questions we ask. Instead we need to let him tell us who he is and what he came to do. We need better questions, not just better answers. I'm reminded here of a once popular bumper sticker that said, "Jesus is the answer!" Within a few months, a non-Christian retort began appearing as well: "What's the question?" I think these folks were actually on to something important.

JESUS REVEALS HIMSELF

JESUS ISN'T JUST THE ANSWER to our questions; he gives us better questions. It's not that our needs are unimportant, it's that they're so shortsighted. We don't know what we really need. Our immediate problems are not necessarily our deepest or our most serious. We focus on the symptoms because they are right in front of us. And they are real: loneliness, abandonment, guilt, fear, depression, broken relationships, and financial or health issues. But Jesus Christ is the answer to the deeper and wider problems that we all face. He did not come just to give us our best life now. He came to give us eternal life. He came to free us from the curse of death and hell and the tyranny of those habits that poison our relationship with God and each other.

The day after Jesus rose from the dead, he found two of his disciples walking along the road, though they did not recognize him at first. In fact, the text tells us that they were *kept* from recognizing him. Jesus struck up a conversation about the recent events in Jerusalem and asked them why they seemed so downcast. They told him, "We had hoped that he [Jesus] was the one who was going to redeem Israel" (Luke 24:21). These disciples held a set of expectations about who the Messiah was and what he had come to do. But the Romans were still in charge and the crucifixion of their teacher had confirmed that tragic reality. They were disappointed and discouraged. But why? Who is Jesus? Whom *should* they have expected?

These disciples along the road to Emmaus needed someone to teach them the Scriptures in order to discover Jesus. So Jesus helped them. He explained to them how the Scriptures prophesied his death and resurrection. In fact, he upbraided them for not knowing these things. His point was not to judge but to show them how the whole Bible—what we call the Old Testament today—proclaimed him as the Savior of Israel and indeed the whole world. Can you imagine the wonder of having the central character of the whole story teaching you how to read the script?

This episode on the Emmaus road underscores the point that even when the risen Jesus was standing before his disciples, the proper way to know him is from "the Scriptures" (Luke 24:27). Why did he keep them from recognizing him? Why didn't he show his hands and side to them and say, "Ta-da! Here I am, risen from the dead"? Of course he later offered his body to the disciples for examination. Thomas put his hands in the holes where the nails and the spear had been driven. Jesus showed them that he was not a ghost. He even asked for some food to eat. Yet on the road to Emmaus, Scripture tells us that the two disciples had been *kept from recognizing Jesus* because the only way to know Jesus, to really know him, is to recognize him as the fulfillment of the Old Testament story.

Accepting their offer of hospitality, Jesus joined the two disciples for dinner. Then he began to take over the house. Upsetting the rules of hospitality, Jesus stood, took the bread, broke it, and gave it to his disciples. These words should sound familiar if you are a Christian. They certainly did to these disciples. This was the formula Jesus had used in the upper room when he instituted the Lord's Supper.

At that point, something changed. They were no longer kept from recognizing him. "Then their eyes were opened and they recognized him, and he disappeared from their sight" (v. 31). I find it fascinating that their first response was to say to each other, "Were not our hearts burning within us while he talked with us on the road and opened the Scriptures to us?" (v. 32). I imagine that I would have been wrapped up in what I had seen—the risen Christ! There is the risen Christ offering the bread and the wine as he did in the upper room! "He is alive—I have seen him with my own eyes!" Yet the point Luke emphasizes is not their witness to the resurrection, but the fact that Jesus wanted them to know him as the risen Savior *from the Scriptures.*

This is essential for us to understand because today *we are in the same position.* Jesus does not offer us his body for inspection or ask us for some fish. Yet he still proclaims himself to us from all the Scriptures. To know Jesus, we have to know the story of which he is the central character.

WHO IS JESUS?

"Jesus is Lord!" These words are not self-explanatory. They can be meaningful and relevant only in the light of the larger biblical story. Otherwise we invoke this phrase simply as a way of legitimizing some other story, such as crying, "Jesus is Lord!" while lopping off the head of an infidel as some did during the Crusades.

Jesus cannot be shoehorned into the story of Christendom or America. He is not a supporting actor in our life movie. He isn't there to be whatever we want—or even think we need—him to be, either personally or as a mascot for the various social and political agendas we have. He will not be reduced to a portrait we have made of him. He has cast us as characters in his story rather than the other way around. And what a story it is! That is why the disciples' sorrow turned to joy.

Jesus the Savior is also God the King. He is Immanuel—*God with us*—who comes to be close to us. "For we do not have a high priest who is unable to empathize with our weaknesses, but we have one who has been tempted in every way, just as we are—yet he did not sin" (Heb 4:15).

Jesus is doubly the king of his kingdom. He is Yahweh, Israel's God. But he is also the faithful Son of David who sits on his earthly father's everlasting throne (2 Sam 7). He is the faithful human king who undoes Adam's unfaithfulness. The whole universe is subjected to the reign of Christ not only as God but also as God's human representative.

It was the blind, the weak, and the sinners who recognized him as the "Son of David" who "comes in the name of the Lord" to deliver his people (Matt 21:9). The religious leaders of Jesus's day, however, didn't see things this way. Jesus exercised his lordship by healing, socializing with moral outcasts, and by preaching good news to the poor. In his parables, Jesus cast the Pharisees as the malicious tenants of the vineyard who killed the prophets and then set their sights on the murder of the master's own son (Luke 20:9–19). As on the day that Israel demanded a king like the other nations instead of God's reign, so too at Golgotha the people rejected Jesus as king and feigned loyalty to Caesar as their motive for handing him over to death.

Yet in his resurrection Jesus became king, not simply as Israel's head of state and commander in chief but as the redeeming ruler of the whole earth. "Who shall separate us from the love of Christ?" (Rom 8:35).

The lordship of Jesus Christ is the lordship of God once again over his kingdom. However, it is not in any way what the religious leaders of his day imagined. Jesus redefined lordship. He redefined kingdom and power and glory. He did so supremely by going to the cross. There he became the laughingstock of the Gentiles

 IMMANUEL: "GOD WITH US"

The angel told Joseph that the fruit of Mary's womb was to be named Jesus—"because he will save his people from their sins" (Matt 1:21). Further, "All this took place to fulfill what the Lord had said through the prophet: 'The virgin will conceive and give birth to a son, and they will call him Immanuel' (which means "God with us")" (Matt 1:22–23, quoting Isa 7:14). What is the crying need of the hour when you're languishing in exile? It is to know that God is among us. Remember the sarcastic query of the unbelieving wilderness generation: "Is God with us or not?" Salvation is a means to a greater end, namely, the presence of God himself in our midst, the ultimate source of everlasting joy, life, and peace.

But it is crucial that we hear these two names—Jesus and Immanuel—together. He is, first, the one who will save us from our sins. Apart from this the announcement of "God with us" could only spell disaster. It would be like the announcement of a plague with us—total disaster. We do not want God showing up on our doorstep. He is majestic in holiness, righteousness, and justice. However, when God comes near to us through Christ's mediation, we have life and blessing—and eternal joy.

and the cursed sinner of the Jews. Yet, raised and exalted, he will be hailed as the King of kings and the Lord of lords by the heavenly host and by Jews and Gentiles alike.

We have already encountered John the Baptist's announcement, "Look, the Lamb of God, who takes away the sin of the world!" (John 1:29). Mary's heart must have been divided between elation at the dawn of redemption and the sorrow of knowing that her beloved son was destined from eternity to die on a Roman cross. This is Jesus's identity from the very beginning of his ministry. Especially in John's Gospel, there are the recurring "musts." Jesus says that he *must* go to Jerusalem. He *must* be put on trial by the Sanhedrin. He *must* be delivered up to the Gentiles and crucified. And only then will he be raised as the beginning of the new creation and exalted to the right hand of the Father.

Jesus is both the Lord who commands and the Servant who obeys. As God he has never stopped ruling the world. But as a human he conquered death, Satan, hell, and sin *as one of us*, flesh of our flesh and bone of our bone. He reigns not only as God but also as the faithful and victorious last Adam. And this means that when he prays for us even now at the Father's right hand, he always has the last word. Satan accuses. He has a damning case against us. But he has been cast forever out of the heavenly courtroom. If you trust in Jesus Christ, you do not have a prosecutor in heaven but only a loving Father who fully absolves you because of the work of his Son.

This is the shape of God's lordship. He rules by serving and serves by ruling. We see this in the intriguing episode of Jesus's washing his disciples' feet (John 13:1–17). It is the night of his betrayal and he will soon be handed over to the Romans, tried, and sentenced to death. Yet before that, as he sits with his disciples in the upper room, he notices that no one has served by doing the customary foot washing. So he takes a towel, kneels, and begins washing the feet of his disciples.

Peter objects: "You shall never wash my feet" (v. 8). Like Peter, sometimes we're too pious for our own good. Peter thought he was being humble. But Jesus replies, "Unless I wash you, you have no part with me" (v. 8). In other words, the first thing in being a disciple—not just at the beginning but throughout our life—is to let Jesus serve us. It is not humble to think you do not need him to serve you with his saving benefits. Christ did not give up his lordship to serve. Rather, he redefined lordship after millennia of sinful distortions by tyrants whose lordship oppressed and dominated. True leadership and authentic lordship are demonstrated by humble service. The greatest in his kingdom is the servant of all.

What King is this who rules not by demanding the life of his subjects for the extension of his empire but by giving his own life for them? Very odd, isn't it? To say that Jesus is Lord is to say that he is sovereign—in charge of everything in heaven and on earth. And yet it is to say so much more. He, not death, is Lord over us. He, not condemnation, has the last word over our destiny. He is Lord not only over Satan and his demonic minions in heavenly places, but over CEOs and dictators, popes and presidents, celebrities and tech gurus. And he is spreading his empire of grace to the ends of the earth, barely noticed by a world distracted by the trivial bells and whistles of this passing age.

BEYOND THE CURSE

"JOY TO THE WORLD!" is a popular song often sung during the Christmas season. But the truth contained in this song is not limited to that season. I especially love the third verse:

> No more let sins and sorrows grow,
> Nor thorns infest the ground;

He comes to make his blessings flow
  Far as the curse is found,
  Far as the curse is found,
  Far as, far as the curse is found.

Our redemption is amazing in its *depth,* but it is also amazing in its *breadth.* The curse that God pronounced as the judgment upon humanity after the fall affects everything. The guilt, corruption, and death that followed disfigure and destroy us. And we see the effects of the fall and of human sin and rebellion everywhere and in every aspect of life.

We turn on others instead of cherishing them. We blame others for our sins. Rebelling against God, we leave violence, injustice, environmental disaster, sexual chaos, and ruined relationships in our wake. Yet the good news is that the blessings of God's redemption will surpass the effects of the curse and the destructive power of human sin. We don't just sing, "Joy to *Me!*" It's good news of great joy to every person and indeed to all creation. The church is that part of the world that has heard and embraced this announcement with joy. And it is the church that sings expectantly of Christ's return for all the world to hear. There is no nook or cranny of this world that will not be restored to righteousness, life, justice, and peace because our Redeemer lives! Even now Jesus is engaged in the work of a new creation, saying, "I am making everything new!" (Rev 21:5; see also 2 Cor 5:17).

As he did in the beginning over the waters of chaos, the Spirit hovers over the darkness and death of our sinful hearts and makes us alive together with Christ (Eph 2:1–5). Through his gift of faith, the Spirit unites us to Christ so that we receive him as our justification and sanctification. Each day the Spirit is renewing us and conforming us to the likeness of Christ (Rom 8:29).

Christ is therefore Lord over all. He exercises this sovereignty not only over creation by his daily providence, but over his church by his saving grace. Every action of the church is a form of witnessing to Christ and ministering Christ to sinners through his means of grace. The Lord does not allow us to defend the faith with coercion and violence. And the main reason for this is the simple fact that we have a gospel to announce rather than a socio-economic-political-legal regime to institute and enforce. Scripture tells us that faith comes by hearing the gospel (Rom 10:17; 1 Pet 1:23–25). Faith is a gift of the Holy Spirit (Eph 2:8–9). You can coerce people to outwardly adopt a creed and pattern of behavior. They may yield assent to certain beliefs. But faith in Christ is a free act of our will as it has been liberated to say its "Amen!" to him and his work for us.

The good news is not an agenda for us to fulfill but an announcement of God's victory in his Son. Therefore we can join the chorus of heavenly hosts as witnesses to that victory to the ends of the earth. We look at the world as it is and, judging by the daily headlines, wonder how much further things can fall apart. "In this world you will have trouble. But take heart! I have overcome the world" (John 16:33). In fact Jesus says, "I will build my church, and the gates of Hades will not overcome it" (Matt 16:18). Here Jesus is clearly on the offensive not the defensive. He is building the church even in and through persecution, wars, distress, famine, and injustice.

It may seem like a stretch of the imagination to picture the church as the official embassy of a king who declares, "All authority in heaven and on earth has been given to me" (Matt 28:18). I say this because the church seems so weak—even sometimes in retreat from the world. Yet Christ is building his kingdom, and he isn't utilizing the means that the world uses to build. Consider that his coronation was with a crown of thorns and his rule was established by his accursed death on a Roman cross. Yet we know that he has the authority to rule because he is the one who was raised from the dead. His resurrection vindicates his claims and gives us the confidence to face death and overcome the world.

In the church, we see people "from every tribe and language and people and nation" being made into "a kingdom and priests to serve our God" (Rev 5:9–10). Even today, as the Word is proclaimed, people are still being "cut to the heart" as they were at Pentecost when Peter preached the gospel (Acts 2:37). The Spirit is still opening hearts. Christ is still welcoming foreigners, sinners, and outcasts to his baptismal bath and royal meal.

BECOMING CHRIST'S DISCIPLE

FROM THIS DRAMA and this doctrine and the doxology that flows from them, the path of discipleship is clear: you need to join a local expression of his church. Christ saves to rule and rules to save. The Bible describes our rebellion against God with the metaphor of wandering sheep, each going its own way (Isa 53:6; 1 Pet 2:25), while Christ the Good Shepherd finds every wayward sheep and brings them back to the security and provision of his fold (John 10:10–16). He does not save his sheep from the wolves only to leave them to fend for themselves.

You need to be not only clothed, bathed, and fed with Christ's saving gifts but taught, guarded, and guided by his ministers and elders. You don't get this online or at a conference or from a book.

Besides the preaching of the Word, baptism lies at the heart of our Lord's Great Commission. Those who heard Peter's message at Pentecost did not sign a card or pray to ask Jesus into their heart. Rather Peter told them, "Repent and be baptized, every one of you, in the name of Jesus Christ for the forgiveness of your sins. And you will receive the gift of the Holy Spirit" (Acts 2:38).

The Lord's Supper is another of God's means of serving us, as a fore-taste of the marriage supper of the Lamb. "Is not the cup of thanksgiving for which we give thanks a participation in the blood of Christ? And is not the bread that we break a participation in the body of Christ?" (1 Cor 10:16). Assuring us of our sharing in Christ, the Supper also strengthens our participation in his body. There are no lone rangers, and before you serve you have to be served.

A *disciple* is one who learns and comes under instruction and guidance. It involves learning through sound teaching and through wise, mature, and godly examples. A disciple is shaped by the prayers of the church both spoken and sung, and by the common confession of sins and of faith in Christ that we make together. Sometimes it means that we need to be corrected in doctrine or life. After all, we are sheep and sheep are prone to wander. Christ loves us too much to let us wander off by ourselves straight over a cliff. If you are united to *Christ*, then you are united to his *body*—his people. You can't be attached to the vine without also being grafted in with the other branches. The local church is essential to being a disciple of Christ.

The church is not only where disciples *go* once a week; it's where disciples are *made*, by the ordinary ministry and the fellowship of the saints. Pastors do not represent the preferences, ideas, and interests of the people, but Christ. Elders are wise in the faith and able to counsel, exhort, and steer the spiritual life of the church. It may run against our individualistic grain, but our King commands, "Have confidence in your leaders and submit to their authority, because they keep watch over you as those who must give an account. Do this so that their work will be a joy, not a burden, for that would be of no benefit to you" (Heb 13:17). We submit to Christ by submitting to his shepherds.

Christ also gives us deacons to serve the temporal needs of Christ's body. God did not create us as disembodied spirits. Nor is he merely in the soul-saving business. Christ has purchased our whole selves—soul and body—and even now cares for our physical as well as our spiritual welfare.

It is through these offices—gifts that Christ gave at his ascension—that we have what we need and can then share our gifts with each other. We may not hold a special office in the church—pastor, elder, or deacon. But we are all priests together, loving and serving each other in Christ's name (1 Pet 2:9). Not only do we need other believers with whom to pray, fellowship, sing laments and praises, and confess; they need us as well. Paul teaches that every part of the body needs the others (Rom 12; 1 Cor 12). We wound Christ's body by our absence but help it to flourish when we participate and use the gifts God has given us (1 Pet 4:10).

No matter how insignificant our churches appear to be in the eyes of the world, they are the consulates of Christ's embassy of grace. Through his apostles, Christ the Lord and Savior calls us to submit to the teaching, fellowship, and discipline of his body. For now, this is where and how his saving lordship is seen and heard. Just as Jesus himself came the first time in humiliation and grief but will come again in glory, the church shares in Christ's suffering for the moment to be revealed at the last as his glorious bride.

Secure in God's fatherly care, we are free to say, "The Lord gives and the Lord takes away; blessed be the name of the Lord." Reason, science, the market, morality, and logic are worthy of our respect precisely because we are no longer enslaved by them. We know now that they are servants and that Jesus is Lord. No matter how irrational and unpredictable God's ways may be to us, he has revealed to us his electing and redeeming grace in Jesus Christ.

We are free to enjoy things we do not need and to give to our neighbors that which they do need for their daily sustenance. We are free to look after our callings, to make wise decisions based on the common knowledge available to us.

Cheered on from the stands by "such a great cloud of witnesses," we "run with perseverance the race marked out for us, fixing our eyes on Jesus, the pioneer and perfecter of faith. For the joy set before him he endured the cross, scorning its shame, and sat down at the right hand of the throne of God" (Heb 12:1–2).

CHAPTER 9

WHAT ARE WE WAITING FOR?

TELL ME WHAT YOU'RE WAITING FOR, and I'll tell you what you love. What gets you up in the morning? The answer is someone or something that you want or desire. Many things can stir our expectations. In the previous two chapters we looked at Jesus and saw that he is the answer to our deepest questions and the fulfillment of the biblical promises. He is the central character of the unfolding plot of world history. And he is the goal, the end to which everything is moving, the fulfillment of our deepest expectations.

Exiled to the isle of Patmos, John, one of the disciples of Jesus and now an apostle and leader in the early church, received a vision. Jesus stood before him and declared, "I am the Alpha and the Omega . . . who is, and who was, and who is to come, the Almighty" (Rev 1:8). Jesus is the beginning and the end or goal, not just of our story but of history itself. This is why he alone was able to open the seals that reveal history's mysteries (Rev 5:2–5).

THE D-BOMB: HOW TO KILL A DINNER PARTY

S O I'LL ASK YOU AGAIN: What are you waiting for? I don't have in mind something like the delivery of your new flat-screen TV, your anniversary getaway, or the next NFL game. I mean, what makes life worth living right now because, somehow, it offers foretastes of the whole purpose of your existence?

There are plenty of cheap answers to that question, even in the religious world. I live in Southern California, where people aren't allowed to die. They just "pass away" like the good old cowboy riding into the sunset. If you want to disrupt a successful party, just drop the "D" bomb: "Hey, how are you doing? Did you know that you and I—all of us here—are going to die someday?" That clears a room pretty quickly. Most people would prefer to talk about how we can have our best life now—with Jesus's help, of course. If all you eat is "chicken soup for the soul," you'll soon find that it is not a healthy diet, especially when the real struggles and difficulties of life come along.

I was recently looking through some obituary clippings about my great-grandfather who was a circuit-riding Methodist missionary. His wife's words summed up his life and death: "Our people die well." What did she mean by that? She meant that believers like my great-grandfather are able to meet tragedy and death not with a cheesy grin but with a wink in the middle of the pain, knowing that for them death has lost its sting. Death is no longer a legal penalty for sin. Death is the burying of the seed in winter that bursts forth from the cold hardness of the earth at Christ's return to flower as part of God's new creation (1 Cor 15:42–45).

Nevertheless, death is not a friend. Death is a real enemy. It is not simply a part of the normal cycle of life. While we rejoice that a deceased loved one is freed from pain and their soul beholds the face of God, we nevertheless hate death. It is an enemy, but it is "the *last* enemy" (1 Cor 15:26; emphasis added). When at last our bodies are raised to share in the newness of Christ's glorified body, we will be forever beyond the reach of God's enemies and ours.

God promises more than a better world or a better you. He promises a *new creation*. This anticipation fills us with more than the ephemeral feeling of well-being that rises or falls with health, wealth, and happiness. It creates joy in our hearts even when we're lying on our deathbed. In fact, I would go as far as to say that Christianity is more about dying than living. I would love to see a "Christian Dying" section next to the "Christian Living" section in the bookstore. What I mean is that, ironically, it is only when we know how to die properly that we finally have some inkling about how to truly live here and now.

Some of the richest devotional literature ever written was by godly men and women who were suffering persecution, succumbing to the flesh-eating ravages of the plague, or experiencing extreme hardship. In past generations there was even an entire literary genre dedicated to teaching people to die well. If you look closely at the beautiful landscapes and still-life paintings of the Dutch masters, you often see a glass of wine half-emptied, scraps of meat, and flowers—like the leftovers of a lavish dinner—with a skull in the background and the words *memento mori* ("remember that you have to die"). They understood something we have largely forgotten: our death is certain.

One characteristic that seems to distinguish us from our pets is our inextinguishable passion to hope. When you have hope, you can endure the direst circumstances. We are by nature prospective creatures. We are always looking ahead to whatever is next on the horizon.

But Christian hope is not a general upbeat attitude. It is not just a positive outlook on life. It is certainly not the modern ideal of progress where the world just keeps getting better and better. Christian hope is generated by the gospel. It is the promises of God fulfilled in Christ that give to believers a unique ability to accept the reality of sickness, weakness, and even death because we know it's not the final chapter.

After explaining that the effects of the curse under which the whole creation groans will be lifted, Paul says, "For in this hope we were saved. But hope that is seen is no hope at all. Who hopes for what they already have? But if we hope for what we do not yet have, we wait for it patiently" (Rom 8:24–25). We know that Paul suffered from chronic illness and weakness. His body had been beaten and scarred, and he had been stoned to the point of being nearly blind. Yet he could say, "For our light and momentary troubles are achieving for us an eternal glory that far outweighs them all" (2 Cor 4:17). Jesus Christ is for people who are dying. (To be clear: that's all of us.)

WHAT HAPPENS WHEN YOU DIE?

YOU CAN TOSS ASIDE the best-selling books that claim to tell you what someone saw in a near-death or after-death experience. These descriptions are nothing more than prosaic accounts of Sunday school imaginations. At numerous points they even contradict what little we are told about heaven in Scripture. "As it is written: 'What no eye has seen, what no ear has heard, and no human mind has conceived'—the things God has prepared for those who love him" (1 Cor 2:9). Whatever is happening in such borderland experiences—chalk it up to continuing brain activity or a subconscious dreamlike state—they are not reliable sources of information about life after death. When people die, they don't come back—not even at Thanksgiving. "People are destined to die once, and after that to face judgment" (Heb 9:27).

Scripture gives us some clues, telling us that when we die, our soul enters God's presence (Pss 16:10; 49:7–15; Eccl 12:7; Luke 16:22; 23:43; 2 Cor 5:8; Phil 1:23; Rev 6:9–11; 14:13). Jesus told the believing criminal on the cross next to him, "Truly I tell you, today you will be with me in paradise" (Luke 23:43), and he himself cried out in his last gasp, "Father, into your hands I commit my spirit" (v. 46). The body apart from the spirit is dead (James 2:26). But for believers, to

 **GOING TO HEAVEN?**

The Bible teaches that at death the souls of believers are immediately present with the Lord. Yet this condition is only temporary as we await the resurrection of our bodies in a new heaven and new earth.

be absent from the body is to be present with the Lord (2 Cor 5:8). This is called the *intermediate state*, which is a good term for this state of our existence. It's intermediate—not final. We are not alive in either the old sense (how we are now) or in the new sense (how we will be forever). We are alive in God's presence but not yet raised in glory.

Many Christians talk about "going to heaven when you die" as if that was the ultimate goal of salvation. But this savors of pagan philosophy rather than biblical teaching. Have you ever noticed the souls before the throne in Revelation 6:9–10? What are they doing? They are not playing harps with chubby toddlers sporting cute wings. Fully aware of the persecutions that their brothers and sisters are experiencing below, they cry out, "How long, Sovereign Lord, holy and true, until you judge the inhabitants of the earth and avenge our blood?" (v. 10). "How long, O Lord?" This was a frequent lament of the Israelites who had been exiled to Babylon. When would God finally vindicate his people and bring justice to the earth? There is a clear sense among these believers that something is still not right. Even in heaven Christ's lordship has not yet been consummated.

Our redemption is not complete until our bodies are raised in immortal glory (Rom 8:23). What Jesus is now, we shall be then. The same Spirit who raised Jesus from the dead is given to us as the guarantee of our sharing in his victory (Rom 8:11). Our culture tries to convince us that our best life is found separate from God and isolated from other human beings in our narcissistic individualism. Our culture is bent on divorce from our Creator, a life separated from the God who made us for himself. But it spills over into all of life, divorcing us from everyone and everything that reminds us of God. It's called "narcissism," but it just turns us into consumers who don't even know why we're alive. By contrast, according to the gospel, salvation means marriage. It is a union of body and soul with God in Christ, uniting people from every nation in a renewed creation as the theater of everlasting joy.

THE FINAL JUDGMENT

JUST THE OTHER DAY a skeptic asked me, "How can you believe in a God who would command the slaughter of innocent people?" He was referring to the destruction of cities and peoples in the book of Joshua during the conquest of Canaan. Reading through the book of Joshua can be tough going at first. If you recall, God's covenant people take the land by force that God had promised to them. But before we judge God or the Israelites, we should be clear that those killed were not "innocent people." In fact, if innocence were the criterion, God's judgment would have been a lot wider. In this episode of the drama, God was declaring war on the idolatrous and violent nations occupying the land that he had sworn to give Abraham's descendants. All the holy wars in the Old Testament are previews of the last battle still to come when Jesus returns to judge the living and the dead.

It is always a mistake to pit the God of the Old Testament—with his wars, judgments, and wrath—against the "meek and mild" Jesus of the New Testament. Why? Because they are the same person. Long before he was made flesh, the Son appeared to Joshua in the form of a man on the battlefield. The surprising figure stood "with a drawn sword in his hand" (Josh 5:13). Understandably, Joshua asked whose side he was on. But the reply was as confusing as the stranger's identity: "Neither . . . but as commander of the army of the Lord I have now come" (v. 14).

That is not the usual response to a question like this. Instead, the stranger tells Joshua, "I am not on anyone's side." In other words, those victories that God won for his people were accomplished by the one standing before Joshua that day with sword drawn. "The commander of the Lord's army replied, 'Take off your sandals, for the place where you are standing is holy.' And Joshua did so" (v. 15). If that last directive sounds familiar, it is because it was the same command that God gave to Moses from the burning bush (Exod 3:5). This is the pre-incarnate Son who rules angelic armies. And the day is coming when he will return to judge the nations. These holy wars were small-scale previews of that great and final judgment, "for [God] has set a day when he will judge the world with justice by the man he has appointed. He has given proof of this to everyone by raising him from the dead" (Acts 17:31).

So if we have trouble with the God of judgment in the Old Testament, we will have even greater reservations about Jesus. They are one and same. When Jesus returns to raise the dead and the whole earth appears before his throne, he will separate the sheep from the goats. The sheep will be welcomed into "eternal life" while the goats will be sent "to eternal punishment" (Matt 25:46).

It is from Jesus that we hear the most vivid descriptions of hell (Matt 5:30; 8:10–12; 13:40–42, 49–50; 22:13; 24:51; 25:30; Luke 16:19–31). In the book of Revelation Jesus announces, "Do not be afraid. I am the First and the Last. I am the Living One; I was dead, and now look, I am alive for ever and ever! And I hold the keys of death and Hades" (1:17–18). In fact throughout the book, Jesus is depicted as the Lamb upon his throne. He is the rider on the white horse who comes in vengeance to destroy his enemies (19:11). He is the judge who will cast Satan and all the ungodly into "the lake of fire" (20:14–15; see also 19:11–20:10).

The same expectation of judgment is found in the New Testament letters. "But because of your stubbornness and your unrepentant heart, you are storing up wrath against yourself for the day of God's wrath, when his righteous judgment will be revealed. . . . There will be trouble and distress for every human being who does evil" (Rom 2:5, 9). In 1 Thessalonians 5 the apostle warns that "the day of the Lord will come like a thief in the night" just when everyone is proclaiming peace and security (vv. 1–3). It will be as final as it is sudden "when the Lord Jesus is revealed from heaven in blazing fire with his powerful angels. He will punish those who do not know God and do not obey the gospel of our Lord Jesus" (2 Thess 1:7–8).

Jude tells us that the destruction we read of Sodom and Gomorrah in the Old Testament is a small picture of what is yet to come. He writes that these cities "serve as an example of those who suffer the punishment of eternal fire" and that false teachers are "wandering stars, for whom blackest darkness has been reserved forever" (Jude 7, 13). Second Peter 3:7 speaks of "the day of judgment and destruction of the ungodly."

Just as God displays both his wrath and his mercy in the Old Testament, so he does in the New Testament. In his first coming, Jesus brought good news. Now is the time of salvation. However, the holy wars of the Old Testament pale in comparison with the judgment that Jesus will bring at his second coming. The former were merely local and limited previews of the universal and final judgment of the world.

HEAVEN ON EARTH AT LAST

HISTORY HAS NEVER BEEN SHORT on utopian dreams. Some have tried to bring about an imagined kingdom of God on earth by force. Others have secularized this vision in bloody revolutions. In fact, tens of millions were murdered brutally in the twentieth century alone in efforts to bring about heaven on earth without God.

Even some Christians suppose that in the end the earth will simply be destroyed. The soul will be freed at last from its bodily prison and enjoy a timeless eternity. But all of these visions of the future are misunderstandings of the hope that is held out for us in Scripture.

Jesus will finally demonstrate his lordship to all people when the dead are raised at the end of the age. Heaven is unspeakably wonderful, but it is not as good as it gets. On resurrection morning, the whole earth will rejoice as it shares with the children of God in their release from bondage to decay, exploitation, bloodshed, and injustice. The whole creation—the earth and its Milky Way galaxy, all the way to the millions of galaxies that have yet to be discovered—will share in this resurrection life that never ends. Heaven is not the opposite of earth. It is not an airy existence that we are promised but an earthy society of love in the presence of the triune God.

Remember that the risen Christ ate fish and dined with his disciples. That is not an insignificant detail. Whatever is true of his resurrected and glorified body will be true of ours as well. At last, the serpent will be driven out of the temple garden. He will not succeed in seeing the plans for God's garden-filled earth fail. In the end it is not the creation that will be destroyed, but all that threatens it. It is not emotions that pass away, but fear and the sound of mourning.

That is why the age to come is compared to a great feast. Isaiah prophesies, "On this mountain the Lord Almighty will prepare a feast of rich food for all peoples, a banquet of aged wine—the best of meats and the finest of wines" (Isa 25:6). There is nothing in that passage about bouncing on clouds as the earth goes up in smoke.

Later in Isaiah we read:

> *Come, all you who are thirsty,*
> *come to the waters;*
> *and you who have no money,*
> *come, buy and eat!*
> *Come, buy wine and milk*
> *without money and without cost. . . .*
> *I will make an everlasting covenant with you. (55:1, 3)*

Amazing, isn't it? No more excommunication, no more being cut off from God and his saving presence. The exile is over. But even more than that, the greater exile from God's presence in death will be taken away from the nations as well. The lion will lie down with the lamb, which is a poetic way of saying that even the peoples who had once been the enemies of God's people will be joined together in one family.

Just as we will have real bodies—the same bodies we were born with though in a radically transformed condition—we will live in a real world of time and space. Remember that God never had any trouble with the creatures. He pronounced it all "good." In whatever ways the creation has been degraded and corrupted, it has humans to thank. But just as creation itself was made to share in the death and disorder of humanity, it will also share in the redemption and glory of the age to come. For this it has another human, God incarnate, to thank.

Some Christians are waiting for destruction. Whenever they see news reports on yet another rogue nation achieving the capacity for making nuclear bombs, they sigh, "Well, Armageddon is pretty near at hand. Good thing we won't be here when the earth is blown up." In their view, there will be a secret rapture of believers, followed by a seven-year tribulation under the cruel scepter of the antichrist. After this, Satan will be bound for a golden age of a thousand years. Then he will be released to wreak havoc again one last time, followed by yet another fall (a rebellion of human beings and angels). Only after the earth is completely destroyed will we live and reign forever with Christ in heaven.

But is this what Scripture says? On the Mount of Olives, Jesus teaches us to expect a long period of wars, earthquakes, and other calamities (Matt 24). "All these are the beginning of birth pains," he says (v. 8). This period began as his followers were persecuted and cast out of the synagogues, and the temple was destroyed by the Romans in AD 70. On the one hand, it will be a period of intense persecution of the church (v. 9). On the other hand, even through persecution the gospel will spread to the ends of the earth. But the end will not come, Jesus says, until the gospel has been proclaimed to all peoples.

Do you see the paradox? We are living in this period that is simultaneously an age of prosperity where the salvation of God is reaching the ends of the earth, yet also an age of tribulation and suffering. The church will thrive in growing and spreading even as the world will become more corrupt and hostile to Christ's kingdom. After this lengthy period, Jesus explains, he will return with his angels to gather his elect from the whole earth and judge the nations.

WHAT'S NEXT?

S O WHAT ABOUT the thousand years mentioned in Revelation 20? Everyone agrees that the numbers in this mysterious vision are symbolic. Ten is a number of completion, so one thousand intensifies the completion. There is no mention in this chapter of a secret rapture, a seven-year tribulation, a war between Israel and her enemies, or a restoration of the theocracy and temple worship in Jerusalem. The book of Hebrews tells us that these old-covenant institutions are fulfilled in Christ and have therefore come to an end. They will not be rebuilt or restored in service to God. Furthermore, in 1 Thessalonians 4:13–18 Paul teaches that, far from a secret rapture that only the believers recognize, Christ's coming for his saints will be a public event attended by trumpet blast. Everyone will witness this event. And the rapture is not separate from the second coming of Christ that begins his everlasting reign, since all that is left after our being "caught up" with Christ when he comes is the everlasting state: "and so we will be with the Lord forever" (v. 17). We live today in joyful confidence because we know how the story ends—or rather—how it *never* ends. As we'll see in the next chapter, this dramatic reversal of fortunes leads us to doxology—praise and thanksgiving—that shapes our discipleship here and now.

In short this is what we are waiting for: the return of Christ to raise the dead, judge the nations, and lead us—with creation in his train—into the everlasting glory of the age to come. So we can say with the apostle Paul, "I consider that our present sufferings are not worth comparing with the glory that will be revealed in us" (Rom 8:18). And we can join in prayer with John's concluding words of the Bible, "Come, Lord Jesus. The grace of the Lord Jesus be with God's people. Amen" (Rev 22:20–21).

CHAPTER 10

IN THE MEANTIME: CALLINGS

I HAVE A TERRIBLE SENSE of direction. So whenever I find myself at the mall, my first stop is the directory with its map and that helpful little phrase: "You are here." When it comes to knowing the times and seasons of God's unfolding plan, we need to know where we are and where we are headed. From Scripture we discover that we are located in a precarious intersection between this present evil age and the age to come. Christ's kingdom is already here but it is not yet consummated. Christ came the first time in humility and self-sacrifice to bring salvation; the second time he is coming in power and glory to judge.

So what should we do in the meantime? There have been three answers to this question. The first answer is *triumphalistic*. We are to transform the world into the kingdom of Christ, using all of our wisdom, resources, and efforts to work to make this world a better place, fit for Christ's return. The second answer is *defeatist*. We are to save souls from the late, great planet earth. The world is going to hell in a handbasket, so we just need to hang on, grab who we can save, and wait for the end. It is pretty easy to land in either one of these places. The third answer puts us in a tougher spot, the place of *witness*. We are to witness to Christ, suffer for that witness, and love and serve our neighbors in our worldly callings. This third answer, which I believe is the biblical one, recognizes the tension between the "already" and the "not yet." In other words, Christ's kingdom is already inaugurated and present, yet we wait patiently for the renewal of all things at the end of the age.

TWO KINDS OF SACRIFICE

THE OLD TESTAMENT LAW provided for two distinct types of sacrifice: *thanksgiving* and *guilt*. The first was natural to our creaturely condition. It served as a tribute offering brought to the great King. It was also one of the things we lost in our rebellion against the King. In Romans, Paul says that the first evidence of our fall in Adam is that we are no longer thankful (Rom 1:21).

After the fall, something else was needed: a guilt offering, a sacrifice to take away sins. It's amazing how this idea of falling short and the gods being angry with us permeates the world's religions. That's why otherwise sane people threw kids into volcanoes, offered someone as an annual sacrifice, and created elaborate schemes to appease the gods or the forces of nature. "If we just do x, then the gods will do y." Yet the good news is that God provides the sacrifice for guilt.

After the fall in Genesis 3, God clothed Adam and Eve with sacrificial skins, pointing to the Lamb of God who takes away the sin of the world. God wasn't bound in any way to do this. It was a sheer act of free mercy on his part. God accepted Abel's sacrifice of the firstborn of his flock but rejected Cain and his offering of the fruit of the earth (Gen 4). Cain not only needed to tip his hat to God as the Lord of the earth but also needed a sacrifice for guilt. The whole sacrificial system of the Old Testament pointed forward to the moment when God the Son, in human flesh, would bear the curse for our sin and bring an end to all sacrifices.

We now live, as those who belong to Christ, in a grace and not a debt economy. We no longer offer sacrifices for guilt. At last, we are free once again to be thankful, to offer ourselves as "living sacrifices" of praise rather than dead sacrifices of guilt. "Therefore, I urge you, brothers and sisters, in view of God's mercy, to offer your bodies as a living sacrifice, holy and pleasing to God—this is your true and proper worship" (Rom 12:1). We're on the receiving end of everything. We're not building a kingdom; we are receiving one. We're not appeasing God; we are receiving his gift of righteousness in his Son. The logic of karma or the law is broken because the God of justice is also the merciful God of grace. The Lord who commands became the Servant who fulfilled the law in our place and now welcomes us into his covenant of grace. *We are passive receivers of the gift of salvation but are thereby made active worshipers in a life of thanksgiving that is exhibited chiefly in loving service to our neighbors.*

There is no divine gift that fails to issue in doxology and no faith that does not yield the fruit of good works. The drama of redemption and its doctrines fill us with the praise and thanksgiving that fuel our discipleship every day.

Notice especially the two crucial points made in 2 Corinthians 1:19–20: "For the Son of God, Jesus Christ, who was preached among you by us . . . was not 'Yes' and 'No,' but in him it has always been

'Yes.' For no matter how many promises God has made, they are 'Yes' in Christ. And so through him the 'Amen' is spoken by us to the glory of God." Jesus Christ alone is the fulfillment of God's promises, and it is only through him that we can say our Amen, which means "Surely it is so!" More than anything else, this is the Christian life. We say in our words and actions that it is surely true that Jesus is the Lord and Savior of the world. The gift has been given. Therefore we are free to give. And what we give is our thanks to God and our good works to our neighbor.

It is crucial that we get this order right. God serves us with his saving grace. We do not offer our good works to God as if he should repay us; rather, all good gifts come down to us from God (Acts 17:25–26; Rom 11:35–36; James 1:17). Then, through us, he serves our neighbors with what they need in daily life. Our good works have nowhere else to go than out to our neighbors who need them.

This means that other people are no longer burdens or threats to our well-being. This implication of the gospel speaks powerfully to our culture of individualism today. Our society tends to look at the elderly or children as burdens to bear, as relationships that leave us drained financially and physically. Or we view our more distant "neighbors" as people to be feared or condemned. We look for scapegoats for everything that's wrong in society. In our sin we tend to divide the world into "us" and "them," and we think that without "them" we'd be doing a lot better.

But the gospel changes all of this. Our well-being is determined by our relationship to Christ, and in Christ our perspective on other people is transformed. We no longer see people as barriers to our happiness or as people to be feared. Through the lens of the gospel we see them as our neighbors, as part of a mutual exchange of gift giving, and not as threats to our well-being.

THE RIPPLE EFFECT OF THE NEW CREATION

B Y HIS WORD, the Spirit is raising those who are spiritually dead and uniting them to Christ through the gift of faith. This means that we are no longer spiritual introverts, focusing on our inner experience, successes, failures, or programs. The good news draws us out into the world, looking up to Christ in faith and out to our neighbor in love and good works. From the preaching of the good news a new community—the society of the age to come—is born into the fading light of this dying age.

The new creation begins with the church, a society within the larger society of the human race. In fact, the fellowship of saints that we experience in the church is even more basic to our identity than our immediate family. Believers are first and foremost brothers and sisters in Christ, and then secondarily they are husband and wife, parents, children, and neighbors. So we find our calling, first of all, among the saints. The apostle Paul compares the church to a body, where each part does its job (Rom 12:3–8; 1 Cor 12:12–27). You may not think that your gifts matter much, but they are essential. The whole body aches when you stub a little finger.

Beyond our identity and calling in the church, there is the family unit. The gospel promise "is for you and your children," as Peter declared in his Pentecost sermon (Acts 2:39). If you are married, then your spouse is your first neighbor. More than that, he or she is your first brother or sister. If you have children, they are also—before anything else—your little brothers or sisters in the kingdom. God gives us different callings and sometimes these change at different points in our life. You may have other callings besides your responsibility to your family, but for a time your main vocation may be to change diapers, teach the faith, and lead family worship.

Beyond the church and the family there are other callings as well. "The promise is for you and your children," Peter says, but also "for all who are far off—for all whom the Lord our God will call" (Acts 2:39). We are called to serve our neighbors, primarily by bringing them the good news of Christ's saving triumph. Beyond these general categories of calling, however, there are many other common callings that we find in the world. Some are called to extend Christ's kingdom directly and full-time, but most of us find our calling by simply providing loving service to others according to the gifts God has distributed. You may have a calling to a profession or to a school or to various neighborhood activities. Perhaps your calling is to feed, clothe, and look after children, driving them back and forth to soccer practice. They are your neighbors who need you. You may design buildings, practice medicine or law, or clean washrooms. All this is what it means for you to be salt and light in a world that would otherwise be completely unaware that it is God's activity through you that makes their lives more meaningful (see Matt 5:13–16).

There is no insignificant calling in Christ's body and there is no role in society that is beneath you. Given the humility of our feet-washing Savior even to the point of the cross, the real question is not *what* is beneath you but *who* is in front of you. When you look outward, God wants you to see your neighbor who needs your gifts of service.

In all of this you must never forget that you don't live for God's approval, much less for the approval of others. God has accepted you in his Son. He has chosen, called, and united you to himself in his Son. He has justified, adopted, and given you his Spirit as a down payment on your final redemption. You don't have to "become somebody" because you *are* somebody—a coheir of Jesus Christ to the divine estate. "Through Christ Jesus the law of the Spirit who gives life has set you free from the law of sin and death" (Rom 8:2). Instead of trying to complete Christ's work, the goal of believers and the church corporately is simply to sing "amen." Instead of trying to transcend nature and history, grace redeems and restores creation. In Christ we are not made more divine but more truly human.

So what should we be found doing on that day when Jesus returns? We should be loving and serving our neighbors by supplying what is needed according to the gifts God has given us. When Christ returns, what do you want him to find you doing? First, you want him to find you *receiving* all of the good gifts that he has to give you from the Father and by his Spirit. You do not want him to find you trying to impress him or to earn his approval. Remember Jesus's parable of the tax collector and the Pharisee. Feigning praise to God, the Pharisee was actually patting himself on the back: "I thank you that I am not like . . ." (Luke 18:11). But the tax collector knew that apart from the mercy of God he was nothing.

Second, knowing that you have everything you need from God, you want Jesus to find you at one of your posts, giving your gifts to others who need them. Wouldn't it be great if he found you taking a sick child to the doctor, feeding your children breakfast, or making love to your spouse? Or filing a report at work, fixing a neighbor's roof, or mopping a floor as a janitor?

FREE TO SERVE

AT THE BEGINNING of this chapter, I mentioned three possible things we can do while we await Christ's return. The first option is to work at transforming the world. With all due respect to your abilities, I will simply say that you cannot do this. It's not within your power. The second option is to give up on the world and to save as many souls as you can before the ship goes down. I hope that you now see that neither of these is a biblical response.

You rejoice in the fact that Christ has toppled the dominion of sin and you see the fruit of the Spirit in your life. Yet you also discern the nagging "fruit of the flesh" that may even make you question sometimes if you are really a Christian. You may receive fresh encouragement from winning one battle, only to face another front of which you were not even aware. But you cannot measure your sanctification.

It is the same in our callings. For the most part we cannot measure our impact. But why should this even matter to us? We have Jesus's promise. *He* has overcome the world. *He* has achieved victory over the world, the flesh, and the devil. *He* is the beginning of the new creation. And *he* will perfect this work when he returns in glory.

In the meantime, we must be clear about our calling. We are called neither to transform society nor to shrink from our responsibilities. In answering the question of what Christians should do in anticipation of Christ's return, the apostle Paul wrote, "Work with your hands, just as we told you, so that your daily life may win the respect of outsiders and so that you will not be dependent on anybody" (1 Thess 4:11–12). We are waiting for that day when Christ returns and makes the kingdoms of this age the kingdom of Christ (Rev 11:15). Until then, we are called neither to change the world nor to abandon it but to love and serve our neighbors to the best of our ability. Sometimes Christians can make a significant and measurable impact on the world around them. Yet our focus should not be on these achievements. It should be on Christ in faith and on our neighbor in love. We do good works not for our status but for the glory of God and the good of others.

Why does this matter? I've found that sometimes new Christians wrongly assume that their life will go better now that they have accepted Christ. But that is not always true. In fact, life can become even more complicated as a Christian. That is because there is a war inside of us between our dominant desire—God and his will—and our indwelling sin, the habits of which have been shaped by our love of the world.

We aren't suddenly immune to sickness or death. We still get sick like everybody else. Our bodies are still dying. For unbelievers, this is a sign of the curse—the everlasting death that awaits them. For believers, it is the "last enemy." No longer a sign of God's judgment, death puts an end to this corrupt body with its evil desires, so that it may be raised in newness of life.

But in terms of outward appearance, our lives—and deaths—are like anyone else's. We share a common curse. Work is often toilsome. Our callings are not always fulfilling even though we have a different set of motives and expectations. Even the pain of childbirth is common to all mothers.

Yet there is also common grace. There is a tendency to think that the Spirit works only with believers. However, Scripture repeatedly reminds us that the Spirit is also at work among unbelievers. Even though they "suppress the truth" in unrighteousness (Rom 1:18–19), unbelievers are restrained in the damage that their unthankful hearts can do. Beyond mere restraint, they too are given gifts that serve not only other unbelievers but believers as well. We benefit from sanitation, from the research and practice of medicine, from the law, government, and the arts. Professing Christians have often been disastrous—even unjust and sinful—in their actions, while unbelievers have often distinguished themselves in service to humanity. All this is due to God's love and care for all that he has made.

Because of God's common grace, Christians can work alongside non-Christians in their callings. To be sure, believers have different motives and goals in doing what they do. Yet when it comes to their methods and their daily vocations, non-Christians and Christians do not seem all that different. Our concern here is not to stand out. We *are* salt and light even if we cannot quantify the difference. Neighbors are served. That is the important thing. And God is the one doing it through believers and unbelievers alike.

HOW CAN YOU KNOW GOD'S WILL FOR YOUR LIFE?

I AM FREQUENTLY ASKED the question: "What is God's will for my life?" Of course, we all want to know our callings. We want to invest our time and energy in the things to which we believe God has called us. However, there is a sharp distinction in Scripture between God's revealed will and his secret plan. We have access to the former but not to the latter. We know the things God has clearly revealed to us in his Word, but we do not have full knowledge of all his plans and purposes.

I grew up in circles where we talked about knowing God's perfect will for our lives. The thinking was based on Paul's words in Romans 12:2: "Do not conform to the pattern of this world, but be transformed by the renewing of your mind. Then you will be able to test and approve what God's will is—his good, pleasing and perfect will." Paul's words here have led some to think that there is a Plan A (God's perfect will) and a Plan B (God's revealed will). They believe that we need to discover God's secret plan for our life so that we pick the right plan, Plan A. But is this really what Paul is saying?

We have to consider the context, which concerns renewal of the mind through God's Word. The context indicates that the perfect will that Paul calls us to discern is *God's moral and saving will insofar as Scripture reveals it.* Therefore, when it comes to the practical decisions we make in life, we are responsible to discern God's will only insofar as it is revealed in Scripture. So while we must marry fellow believers (2 Cor 6:14), other considerations regarding our spouse are left to our wisdom, the counsel of friends, and the desires of our hearts. Although God has "marked out [our] appointed times in history and the boundaries of [our] lands" (Acts 17:26), we have no way of discovering the details that God has kept hidden. So God's good, acceptable, and perfect will is what he has revealed in his Word. And by this Word we are being transformed each day through the renewing of our mind. In this Word he reveals his moral will (the law) and his saving will (the gospel). This means that everything God says that we need to know is contained in Scripture. Beyond that, God's secrets are just that—secret.

This also means that we must learn to become wise and discerning. God does not gift us for things we cannot do well unless he also gives us the mentors and opportunities to learn them. Otherwise, God leaves it up to us to seek the help of those who know us and his Word well enough to offer godly counsel. Some readers may recall the 1981 film *Chariots of Fire*. In the movie, the Christian character Eric Liddell has planned for years to be a missionary with his sister. But he also has a desire to run. When he senses that he wants to run in the Olympics, he says to his sister, "God also made me fast. When I run, I feel his pleasure."

You may not always "feel his pleasure" in your calling. You may feel nothing but the residue of a half-eaten dinner underneath your fingernails after washing the dinner plates for the thousandth time. But sometimes there is also that sense of, "Hey, this is what God made me for." And it may not be just one thing. We must see that God makes us for all sorts of different callings. You don't just choose one calling. You choose many over a lifetime. So go with the set of gifts and sense of God's pleasure that fits with your life right now. Don't worry about the other callings—especially those that may lie in the future. Just be who God has called you to be right where you are, with the people he has called you to serve. You will make a difference, but life is not about making a difference. It is about doing what God has made you to do so that you can be a conduit of his love and service to others.

Do you see how liberating this message is in a world that schemes and strives fruitlessly to liberate itself? The *drama* of redemption is the good news that we need every day. We do not ascend to God. He descended to us, assuming our humanity. Jesus Christ fulfilled all righteousness for us and bore our judgment. He was raised to the right hand of the Father as the beginning of the new creation. With the Father, the victorious Christ sent his Spirit to raise us from spiritual death and to indwell us as the guarantee of our bodily resurrection.

All saving benefits come from the Father, in the Son, through the Spirit. We receive his law and his gospel regularly. We not only hear the faith-creating promise again and again, but God ratifies his pledge visibly in baptism and the Lord's Supper.

We become shaped together by this *drama* and by the *doxology* that it yields in common prayer and praise. And then we live as those who are not their own but belong to Jesus Christ. "What, then, shall we say in response to these things? If God is for us, who can be against us?" (Rom 8:31).

So then where do our good works go? They go out to our neighbors who need them. We are called to a *discipleship* that grows out of living on the Vine—in union with Christ and together with the communion of saints. Then God gives us gifts, not only for fellow believers but for those who do not yet know Christ. He makes us his ambassadors, conforming us to the image of his Son, witnessing by word and deed to Christ's victory over sin and death. "Therefore, I urge you, brothers and sisters, in view of God's mercy, to offer your bodies as a living sacrifice, holy and pleasing to God—this is your true and proper worship" (Rom 12:1).

So give up whatever script you may be working on for your life movie. Dig into God's script and the Holy Spirit will cast you as a character in the greatest story ever told. This is core Christianity.

AFTERWORD
TYING IT ALL TOGETHER

ARE YOU RELIGIOUS? I ask because for most people religion is mainly about what they feel or do. It is *subjective*. It is not something found in the realm of reason and knowledge, but a matter of inner experience and morality. As I have argued in this book, our experience and our morality are certainly crucial aspects of being a Christian. And there is also our doxology—both our confession of sin and our praise for salvation. And this in turn gives rise to a new way of living in the world—discipleship.

Yet all of this—our thanksgiving and obedience, our experience and morality—are based on something objective. It is based on a historical drama and doctrines that are objectively true regardless of what we feel or do.

The heart of Christianity is a *gospel*, an announcement of good news. Among other things, this means that *the* faith—the truth—comes before *our* faith—personal experience and decision. Of course we are saved through faith in Christ and this is something we must subjectively experience, but it is only possible because Christ has accomplished our redemption outside of us, two thousand years ago, in the precincts of Jerusalem.

Everything we've explored thus far underscores the *objective* truth of the Christian faith:

→ God is not an inner feeling of empowerment, but the triune God who exists eternally regardless of whether he had chosen to create the universe and us as part of it.

→ Human beings are objectively glorious as God's image and likeness and are objectively guilty and corrupt since the fall.

→ Christ is not just a great man who experienced a closeness to God but the eternal Son who assumed our humanity. His life and death cancelled God's objective condemnation, not just our feelings of guilt. He died not just to show us how much God loves us so that we will love him back, but to bear our curse as an objective sacrifice for sin. Sometimes we may not have "that peaceful, easy feeling" about which the Eagles sang, but the gospel announces to us an objective "peace with God" through Christ's blood (Rom 5:1). By his resurrection Jesus not only made it possible for us to live a happier and healthier life; he destroyed the reign of sin and death.

→ The Holy Spirit is not a feeling, but a person—the third person of the Trinity—who raises us from spiritual death, changes us, and will raise our bodies from death in resurrection.

→ Preaching, baptism, and the Lord's Supper are not just opportunities for our reflection, remembering, and rededication. They are God's objective acts through which he saves and sanctifies his people.

→ The church is not merely a voluntary society of people who share a similar experience. It is the royal embassy of the King of heaven. Throughout our whole life we are being immersed in the story of God in Jesus Christ, through the power of the Spirit, in the communion of the saints. The gospel is the true story and our discipleship is a process of "getting in character," taking up the lines and actions that are called for in this new script we have been given.

→ Finally, Christ will return bodily. This is not a metaphor for our spiritual ascent through contemplation and service. Our Savior will be just as objectively present among us at this time as he was when he was held by the Virgin Mary and when he hung upon a cross.

In a world where most religions emphasize how we feel or what we do, Christianity stands apart. At the core of the Christian faith are objective, historical realities that secure our faith. And with our salvation fully secured, we are able to look up in faith toward God and out to our neighbor in love. We are part of a new creation, being swept up in the train of Christ's resurrection from the dead. It is this history of Jesus and not that of this age that is the real rudder of destiny—both the story of the world and the story of our own lives. Christ has died, Christ is risen, and Christ will come again.

NOTES

1. C. S. Lewis, *Mere Christianity* (London: Collins, 1952), 54–56.
2. John A. T. Robinson, *The Human Face of God* (Philadelphia: Westminster, 1973), 131.
3. Paul L. Maier, "Josephus and Jesus," *4Truth.Net*, http://www.4truth .net/fourtruthpbjesus.aspx?pageid=8589952897. Paul Maier, a professor of ancient history, is the editor and translator of *Josephus: The Essential Works*, rev. ed. (Grand Rapids: Kregel Academic, 1995). He recognizes that Josephus's affirmation of Jesus as the risen Lord (in *Jewish Antiquities* 18:63) in standard collections may be a later Christian insertion. He observes, however, that Professor Schlomo Pines of Hebrew University discovered a different manuscript tradition of this work that more likely represents the original. This tradition is what is quoted here (*An Arabic Version of the Testimonium Flavianum and Its Implications* [Jerusalem: Israel Academy of Sciences and Humanities, 1971]).
4. Samuel Sandmel, *A Jewish Understanding of the New Testament*, 3rd ed. (Woodstock, VT: Jewish Lights Publications, 2010), 33.
5. Herman Bavinck, *Reformed Dogmatics: God and Creation*, ed. John Bolt; trans. John Vriend (Grand Rapids: Baker, 2004), 2:260. It should be noted that I am discussing the Trinity after the attributes not because God's unity is more important than his plurality, but because it makes sense to discuss first the characteristics that each person shares as God.

6. Quoted from Arius's poem "Thalia" as found in Rowan Williams, *Arius: Heresy and Tradition* (Grand Rapids: Eerdmans, 2002), 102.

7. Gregory of Nazianzus, *Oration 40: The Oration on Holy Baptism* 41 (*NPNF2* 7:375).

8. This point is ably argued in relation to the Spirit by Gordon Fee, *God's Empowering Presence: The Holy Spirit in the Letters of Paul* (Peabody: Hendrickson, 1994).

9. Based on the assumption that the Bible is not clear enough, the Roman Catholic Church teaches that only an infallible teacher can explain it. But history simply does not bear out that this grand idea has ever been achieved.

10. Robert Jay Lifton, "The Protean Style," in *The Truth About the Truth: De-Confusing and Re-Constructing the Postmodern World*, ed. Walter Truett Anderson (New York: G. P. Putnam's Sons, 1995), 130–40.

SCRIPTURE INDEX

SUBJECT INDEX

organism called, 78
persecution of, 155
church history, doctrine in, 44
common grace, 165
Communion, *See*, Lord's Supper
compassion, 59–60
confession, of sins, 141
Council of Chalcedon, 35
covenant
    and eschatology, 83–84
    curses and blessings, 115
    of creation, 91
    terms of the, 103–104
creation, 55, 63
    covenant of, 91
    creator and his, 83
    into existence, 82
    and the Trinity, 43
crucifixion, 31
curse, beyond the, 137–38
curses, and blessings, 115

Daniel, 100
David, 100, 110–14
Davidic covenant, 110–14
deacons, 141
death, 57
    expectation of, 90
    immunity to, 165
    life after, 149

has lost its sting, 146–48
moving toward, 87
depravity, 94–95
disciple
    Christ's, 140
    one who learns, 141
    witnesses to Christ, 37
discipleship
    and faith, 17
    and good works, 18
    called to, 168
    path of, 140
divorce, 150
Docetism, 34, 36
doctrine
    in church history, 44
    matters, 13–19
    of the Trinity, 40–52
doxology
    faith in terms of, 17
    "praise," 18
drama
    form of, 20
    informed by doctrine,
        18–19
    to doctrine, 34
    unfolding, 17

Ebionites, 35, 36
eschatology, covenant and, 83–84

essence, God is one in, 41, 48, 50
eternity, 55
evil
    distortion of, 88
    in the world, 61–66
    problem of, 89–91
evolution, 13
expectations, fulfillment of, 145
experience, 169

faith
    and reason, 15–16, 21
    gift of, 139
faithfulness, 59, 61
fall, the, 158
family, 162
Father, the
    and Jesus, 41
    worship of, 51
freedom, human, 58, 61, 64

genres, in the Bible, 102–103
Gentiles
    and the gospel, 26
    Jews and, 24, 74
    Paul's mission to, 42
    worldview of, 45
gifts
    from God, 160, 168
    giving one's, 163

that Christ gave, 142
God
    character of, 54
    great and good, 53–66
    Jesus is, 23
    speaks, 67–71, 82
    study of, 20
    three persons, 39
    transcendence of, 13
    will of, 166
good news. *See*, gospel
gospel, the, 16, 169
    announcement of, 96
    heart of, 127–28
    meaning of, 19
    preaching of, 69
    proclaimed, 155
    spreading of, 121
Great Commission, the, 140
Greeks, seek for wisdom, 45
Gregory of Nazianzus, 50
guilt, 158–59

heaven
    in Scripture, 148–50
    on earth, 153–55
hell, descriptions of, 151–52
Herod the Great, 122
history
    doing, 33

God works within, 119
holiness, 59–60
Holy Spirit, the
    carried along by, 73
    casting director, 18
    continued to lead, 107
    gift of, 139
    indweller, 39
    of the Trinity, 40–52
    worship of, 51
hope, 148
human, means to be, 82–91
human beings, 84
humanity
    essence of our, 94
    in Adam, 91
hypostatic union, 34, 35

idolatry, 88
image of God, 84
Immanuel, 135
immorality, 88
immutability, 55–56
individualism, 150, 160
inerrancy, 73, 76
inspiration, 73
intermediate state, 149
Israel
    nation of, 116
    story of, 25–26

jealousy, 59–60
Jehovah's Witnesses, 35, 48
Jesus Christ, 119
    asked his disciples, 36
    born, 119
    claimed to be God, 27
    death of, 30
    genealogy of, 121
    God, 23
    greater Joseph, 130
    identity of, 23–26
    Lord, 131
    and the Old Testament, 101
    reveals himself, 132–33
    unfolding plan in, 77
    who is, 134–37
    Yahweh, 28
Jews
    and Gentiles, 24, 74
    demand signs, 45
    "stumbling block," 26
Jezebel, 113
John the Baptist, 126, 136
Joseph, 100
    the greater, 130
Josephus, 31
Joshua, 108–109
joy, to the world, 117
judgment
    expectation of, 90

the final, 150–52

justice, 59–60

justification, 129, 138

law, the
    and the gospel, 128
    given to Adam, 90
    given to Moses, 107
    requirement of, 29
    works of, 68–69

leadership, true, 137

Lewis, C. S., 29

Lord, Jesus is, 29, 131

Lord's Supper, the, 141

lordship, of Jesus Christ, 135

love, 59–60

marriage, 89

Mary, 118, 136

mercy, 59–60

Messiah, 31, 36, 37, 119

modalism, 46–48

Monophysitism, 36

morality, 169

Mormonism, 35, 48

Moses, 100, 106–110

narcissism, 150

neighbor, 161–62

Nestorianism, 35, 36

new covenant, 78, 115, 130

new creation, effect of the, 161

Nicaea, 48

Nicene Creed, the, 49

old covenant, 129

Old Testament, the
    making sense of, 100–102
    the Trinity and, 42

omnipotent, 58

omnipresent, 57

omniscient, 57

oppression, 88

Origen of Alexandria, 46

original sin, 91–95

Paul, the apostle, 26
    and the Gentiles, 42

Pelagius, 92

Pentecost, 45

perichoresis, 50

persecution, 139
    of the church, 155

Peter, 136–37

Plato, 46

polytheism, 40

prayers, 141

preaching, as public scolding,
    68–69

Spirit, hovers, 138. *See also*, Holy
   Spirit
story, Christians and their, 14
subordinationism, 46
suffering, 155

temple, the, 111, 115
Ten Commandments, the, 29,
   107
thanksgiving, 158–59
theology, 16
   engaging in, 20. *See also*,
      doctrine
tomb, empty, 31
total depravity, 94–95
tree of life, 97
tribulation, 155
Trinitarian Theism, 40
Trinity, the
   doctrine of, 39
   the Old Testament and, 43

truth, 169–70

unity, 55–56

verbal-plenary inspiration,
   73–74
violence, 89

will, of God, 166
witness, to Christ, 158
Word
   giving birth to the church,
      78
   preaching of the, 68–71
   revelation of God in, 167.
      See also, Bible; Scripture
worldview, 20, 40

Yahweh, 134
   Christ as, 28

For Calvinism

Michael Horton

The system of theology known as Calvinism has been immensely influential for the past five hundred years, but it is often encountered negatively as a fatalistic belief system that confines human freedom and renders human action and choice irrelevant.

Taking us beyond the caricatures, Michael Horton invites us to explore the teachings of Calvinism, also commonly known as Reformed theology, by showing us how it is biblical and God-centered, leading us to live our lives for the glory of God.

Horton explores the historical roots of Calvinism, walking readers through the distinctive known as the "Five Points," and encouraging us to consider its rich resources for faith and practice in the twenty-first century.

As a companion to Roger Olson's *Against Calvinism*, readers will be able to compare contrasting perspectives and form their own opinions on the merits and weaknesses of Calvinism.

Available in stores and online!

Pilgrim Theology

Core Doctrines for Christian Disciples

Michael Horton

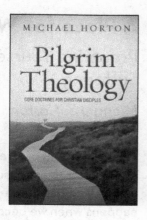

The 2011 award-winning publication *The Christian Faith* garnered wide praise as a thorough, well-informed treatment of the philosophical foundations of Christian theology, the classical elements of systematic theology, and exegesis of relevant biblical texts. *Pilgrim Theology* distills the distinctive benefits of this approach into a more accessible introduction designed for classroom and group study.

In this book, Michael Horton guides readers through a preliminary exploration of Christian theology in "a Reformed key." Horton reviews the biblical passages that give rise to a particular doctrine in addition to surveying past and present interpretations. Also included are sidebars showing the key distinctions readers need to grasp on a particular subject, helpful charts and tables illuminating exegetical and historical topics, and questions at the end of each chapter for individual, classroom, and small group reflection.

Pilgrim Theology will help undergraduate students of theology and educated laypersons gain an understanding of the Christian tradition's biblical and historical foundations.

Available in stores and online!

A Place for Weakness

Preparing Yourself for Suffering

Michael S. Horton

In a world of hype, we may buy into the idea that, through Jesus, we'll be healthier and wealthier as well as wiser. So what happens when we become ill, or depressed, or bankrupt? Did we do something wrong? Has God abandoned us?

As a child, Michael Horton would run up the down escalator, trying to beat it to the top. As Christians, he notes, we sometimes seek God the same way, believing we can climb to him under our own steam. We can't, which is why we are blessed that Jesus descends to us, especially during times of trial.

In *A Place for Weakness*, formerly titled *Too Good to Be True*, Horton exposes the pop culture that sells Jesus like a product for health and happiness and reminds us that our lives often lead us on difficult routes we must follow by faith. This book offers a series of powerful readings that demonstrate how, through every type of earthly difficulty, our Father keeps his promises from Scripture and works all things together for our good.

Available in stores and online!

ZONDERVAN®
.com

Ordinary

Sustainable Faith in a Radical, Restless World

Michael Horton

Radical. Crazy. Transformative and restless. Every word we read these days seems to suggest there's a "next-best-thing," if only we would change our comfortable, compromising lives. In fact, the greatest fear most Christians have is boredom—the sense that they are missing out on the radical life Jesus promised. One thing is certain. No one wants to be "ordinary."

Yet pastor and author Michael Horton believes that our attempts to measure our spiritual growth by our experiences, constantly seeking after the next big breakthrough, have left many Christians disillusioned and disappointed. There's nothing wrong with an energetic faith; the danger is that we can burn ourselves out on restless anxieties and unrealistic expectations. What's needed is not another program or a fresh approach to spiritual growth; it's a renewed appreciation for the commonplace.

Far from a call to low expectations and passivity, Horton invites readers to recover their sense of joy in the ordinary. He provides a guide to a sustainable discipleship that happens over the long haul—not a quick fix that leaves readers empty with unfulfilled promises. Convicting and ultimately empowering, *Ordinary* is not a call to do less; it's an invitation to experience the elusive joy of the ordinary Christian life.

Available in stores and online!

THE CAMPAIGN FOR
CORE CHRISTIANITY

The gospel is nothing less than "the power of God that brings
salvation to everyone who believes . . ." (Romans 1:16).
Not even the gates of hell can prevail against the church as
believers become confident in the truths of God's Word.

Today we stand at a historic crossroad. The joy, hope, and confidence
of Jesus Christ that comes from this gospel is rapidly disappearing
under the crush of a culture of disbelief. Many don't know what
they believe or why they believe it. We often respond by making
the church more like the world or channeling the latest marketing
gimmicks instead of focusing on what Christ has accomplished.

The Campaign for Core Christianity is dedicated to helping
the body of Christ transform their story from being about
themselves to being about God. When we understand what the
Bible teaches, we can all find ourselves in God's story.

Join the campaign and find yourself in God's story. Visit
our website and become part of the conversation.

CORECHRISTIANITY.COM